LETTERS TO
LODIETA

To,

BRENDA,

MY LONG TIME FRIEND

THIS FOOLISH HALF BLIND MAN HAS
ACTUALLY PUBLISHED A BOOK! LAUGH OUT LOUD

LETTERS TO LODIETA

A COLLECTION OF VERSE

IAN WILCOX

Rev. date: 04/25/2018

To order additional copies of this book, contact:
Xlibris
800-056-3182
www.Xlibrispublishing.co.uk
Orders@Xlibrispublishing.co.uk
778589

CONTENTS

FLOATING MARBLES

Floating Marbles 3

A Pilgrim of the Alter Ego 4

The tribe of Lovers 6

Mendips, Monuments and mystic Marvels 7

Admin Army 9

Empire Son 11

Little Man 12

The fable of the Fox cub 14

A Toast to Tantric tumbles 16

Bad day (melee of the morning meal) 17

Billy the Banjo 18

Carnivals and Celebrations 20

Puzzle pieces 21

A 'rich kids' story 22

Came a Virgin 23

His promise kept 25

Choral chant of the Modem masses 29

Today I dream of Avalon 31

The Desert of Life 33

Amazon Echoes 34

Baked this morning 36

Behind sad eyes 37

Cupid, Mars and Aphrodite 39

"Ello Mister" 41

Aspirations take hiatus 42

Cedric Snowman 44

Bubbling Brook 45

The candid Kid 46

And I remembered 48

Drive...50
Accent the aspiring actions...51
Changed the River 53
Tri Colour merge...54
The family of mother Life 56
Born inside you 57
Pegasus..58
Simple 60
Raise my Glass 61
Before too old..62
A start 63
Celeste 64
To create a person...65
Mystery Blue 67
Cleansing 68
The Dark 70
The Family..71
Come Sunday come Sleep day 73
Midnight Rising...75
Consequences of conscious conscience.........................76
The Dream speaks 78

LOVE

Bounce, bounce...81
The Prize..82
Mini You and mini me...83
Love across the Oceans..84
Two Ships 85
Number One..86
Utopia within your Kiss 87
Lodieta my Special Rose..88
Yes...90
When the Love is strong..91

Strawberry Sun..93
Paint for me the perfect Picture....................................94
When Two Hearts...95
Jericho Wall and Lodieta..96
I saw your Face, I saw the future 98
Side by side...100
When I have the words..101
And spend the days together..102
Breaking Walls..104
Eyes...106
L.Y.F..108
Call of the Wild...109
Link of Gold 111
Touch the Heavens...112
Met in mellow moving cloud...113
Can't feel down 115
Sweetest..116
Chains and Walls 117
In time of joy 118
Beside you...122
In warm Moonlight...124
That holds your Head 126
Closer...127
Golden 128

LIFE

The Poet with the Stick..133
In some M.i.a place 135
Someday Maybe..137
I swam with Dolphins – and do again..........................138
Soul Spirits...142
Plastic Eyes...143
'Man Flu' 144

Golden Star 145

Heart Attack 147

7 Seas 148

Born one place 149

Afterglow 151

Footfalls of forgotten foes 153

Let soft Music play 154

Natures Rubber 155

Fiddle me dumb 156

Am I 157

At First 158

A eulogy to life 160

Across the Miles - Communication, narration 162

Left of seat 164

Back to what one was 166

Cherries or Prunes 168

Random Objects and Nodding Dogs 170

Go Crazy 171

Before me 173

Pipe and Harp 175

By Heck 177

Sparrow's Fart 178

Sunday Dilemma 179

Alas regrets but forever grateful 180

Green Sleeves and running Nose 182

The Tear Drops turn to Crystals 184

Dear Self 185

THOUGHT

Alba 189

Begin... 191

Whirly Bird... 192

Drifting... 194

Pure White Dove 195
Wind of change...196
Had a Penny..197
The Father of my Father...198
A Rhapsody...199
Bus and Ferry..201
Polaris 203
Cappuccino Prose... 204
Silence is Golden 205
Bad start..206
Born as normal...207
This road we travel...209
Browning 211
Cauldron..212
Can I be a Rainbow?... 214
Tick Tock beats the Clock.....................................216
Aspiring Man.. 218
Breath away..220
Milk and Honey...221
Because of you..222
Chill...224
A Life fulfilled...225
Sunken Seeds 227
Can you see? 228
When elders speak..230
Angels rode on Horseback.....................................231
Carry me along 233
Be this way...235
When Angels fly 237
Can it be?...238
Bee...240
Alcoholic attitudes...241

To my love and Soul mate Lodieta J Sumayo
We might be currently parted physically
but we are always together

Forever and a Day

The couple lay arm in arm
Staring at the night
Counting stars in black velvet sky
Twinkling pure and bright
"Will you be mine forever?" she said
In a voice serene
"No" he said as he looked at her
"For that the end does mean
Finality is not a word
That we should care to use
Ending has a sorry taste
Not a feeling that I choose
We will last for a much longer time
We'll go on past forever
Infinite is our mutual love
For it does have no measure
Some loves last forever true
But listen to what I say
While that is fine for other people
Ours will last forever and a day"

FLOATING MARBLES

FLOATING MARBLES

I am a Freak of that I know
My thinking is mislead
For instead of Brain from sense to gain
I've a Centrifuge instead

No top has got so no lid to stop
The contents whirling and then flying
Which way they go I don't know
Leave some poor souls just crying

For I've got (and a lot)
Floating Marbles instead of thought
So catch I plead if indeed
They are witnessed and can be caught

My World a Kaleidoscope
Of colour in the clear
Some are wild like untamed child
Some thoughtful and so dear

Join with me and try to see
The objects of their kind
For help I need so true indeed
For me I am half blind

Please gather up and send them back
To where they do belong
For my Doctors say (though somewhat astray)
They will help me to get strong

A PILGRIM OF THE ALTER EGO

A shadow figure upon the Stage
Had many a record of when came of age
Many a story about what had done
Many a character in Body one

Some self invented
Some just rumours
Some for friends
Some Business suitors

Went on so long that none could tell
Self grandeur or protection shell
In front of many they plied their trade
For the masses shows they made

They were a Pilgrim of the Alter Ego
Worshipping both Day and Night
Got confused at who was true
Became immune between wrong and right

Soon the characters began to bleed
Found that both they did need
One was normal but itinerant
One eccentric and quite brilliant

A stable life so hard to find
When are two people of different kind
"Switch off/ Switch on - or be both and carry on?
Do I know if here belong?"

Repeated this daily did the Pilgrim
Which should stay now which should go?
A complex state of complex man
One minute Frank, then Fernando

Some said self inflicted
Some said an accident
Some said he was buried deep
Some said Astral Stage he went

I am not sure for didn't know him
Though have heard of others of his kind
A Pilgrim of the Alter Ego
Too many paths for just one Mind

THE TRIBE OF LOVERS

We care to want and want forever
We come alone but leave together
We share a hope and share a bed
You stay with me inside my head

We touch and feel in gentle motion
We both know and have that notion
Share our thoughts and share our dreams
We count the cost of in between

We trade in love and love so deep
Trade in feelings that we keep
We love again and do move on
Search again when it has gone

We take and give then give again
We feel again but know not when
Something deep between the covers
We are the tribe, the tribe of lovers

MENDIPS, MONUMENTS AND MYSTIC MARVELS

Mendip peak, pure location
To the tourists that tales seek
Jutting up from soils richness
Finding out the climber weak
Somerset the morning wakens
Land of cider and Cricket Team
Yet the Mendips scaled and conquered
Live inside so many a dreams

Square cones of stone, smoothed and honed
From the sands do rise
Heated air with Suns' hot stare
Another's form of Paradise
Spitting beasts with mood released
Sway and rock you to the place
Now stripped and looted of those commuted
Those embalmed with masked face

The cliff dwellings of Mesa Verde
Snapshots of a different past
Gone the dwellers and story tellers
Yet the silence makes the cast
Walk in wonder within the vacuum
Reflect on life a grand ago
How was the thinking of the people?
When our future they did not know

Me, as English, loves Stonehenge
Mix of cult and need to ask
Why and how did they build it?
Was alignment chance or was it task?
Still today we live in wonder
Of ancient things we cannot measure
Protected now for preservation
Now appreciate a National Treasure

Mendips, Monuments and mystic marvels
Uncluttered spaces that we can go
Gaze and wander in deep thinking
Of the people we hardly know
Yes we have an insight
Yes we have some clue
Though the language spoken by artefacts
Differs greatly from me and you

ADMIN ARMY

Bugle sounds they call Alarm clock
Up, showered, dressed then bite to eat
Check phone battery strong then top layer on
Out of there to massed commuters feet

Queue for Transport of your choice
Squeeze in tight, no room to breath
After cancellations and delays
Maybe squashed but with relief

For you're in the army now
The Admin Army of this land
Bums on seats for monotonous feats
The uninformed say it's grand
Same four walls, same type of calls
All expecting attentive voice
While they're irate and you berate
As if it was your choice

Small talk with soldiers just like you
When for five minutes can grab a brew
The time does drag til lunch
You feel berserk yet still you work
The spreadsheet numbers crunch

After what seems days the roster says
Furlough for short while
Some eat in place but you need space
That's really not your style

Too soon the gloom of afternoon
As you drop back to your station
The things you do to get us through
Us ungrateful of the Nation

———

For you're in the army now
The Admin Army of this land
Bums on seats for monotonous feats
The uninformed say it's grand
Same four walls, same type of calls
All expecting attentive voice
While they're irate and you berate
As if it was your choice

At long last you've finished task
If only for one day
Again the crush as Commuters rush
Back Home rest and play

Oh sublime but short the time
That can call your own
Before again the Bugle pain
Back to workplace clone

One day you'll leave but no-one will grieve
For it's just for another posting
Within a week your replacement seek
Will hire and to them Toasting

For you're in the army now
The Admin Army that's self replacing
They don't care for there's someone out there
To do what you are facing
They can swell the ranks but give no thanks
For the effort you put in
Or cut their costs with positions lost
In new Regiment you must begin

EMPIRE SON

A man was born into a nation
His experience had just begun
A history so full of 'glory'
A child of the empire of eternal sun

A 'proud' history through misted eyes
For was successful within its past
Those days are gone but not forgotten
Deeds were done and deeds do last

When 'might was right' and it mattered
When occupation was a king
Subjugation was a necessity
No thought spared for what will bring

Yet a man was born into a nation
Proud and strong is life begun
He belongs in a proud nation
He is regarded as an empires son

The man grew older and realised
The prophecy did have no chance
The nation had 'paid its piper'
But nation bold did know not dance

The empire son did stop and laugh
For he could see the irony
You ruled and conquered for so many years
Now reap the rewards that you did not see

LITTLE MAN

A lonely Boy walks down a lonely road
No friends to wash his clothes
Always looking to the future
The past for him is all he knows
But he has dreams, he has ambitions
He's faced barriers too many times before
Determination and endurance, he has the bravery to explore
And the little man will move on

The future is sponge – floating Marbles
Bouncing within a challenged mind
Hidden walls and barriers
Until your path and reason find
Imagination should rule supreme
His knowledge will fight through
Banish all the Demons lurking
Let the truth shine bright and true
The little man could dream

Through adolescence he never fitted
Not the warmth of a velvet glove
He endured it all and journeyed onwards
But what he missed was a thing called Love
Goals and ambitions kept him sane
He stretched and reached a higher plane
Ever dogged in his ambition
He found emotion in a different name
The little man wrote

Now the Boy has become a Man
Comfort rests in what he has become
Lays at rest without the Demons
Has found the joy of the number one

Does not seek to share his world
No-one he thinks would understand
Social to others when he wishes
But solace is a life so grand
The little man is secure in his life

He is a being of noble virtue
He is a man of thought and care
A product of a different up bringing
He just missed out on what was not there
But a man all the same
Lives and breathes, bleeds when cut
Laughs and jokes when he feels happy
Withdraws and ponders when in a rut
Little man is Human

He wakes each morning and greets the sunrise
He has contentment in who he is
Purpose and conviction scream out true
To realise is truly bliss
Like all around he is no different
Casual amongst the maddening crowd
But different in a chosen way
His convictions solid and scream out loud
Little man has become a rock

Life is all about future experiences
Not looking back on what has gone before
Ambitions to reach, dreams to realise
Life is but an open Door
Little man now feels a Giant
Not in size but in what he has become
From a nothing with no future
He broke the locks shackles came undone

I.Wilcox

THE FABLE OF THE FOX CUB

The young Fox cub paced the Den
It was bored and sought to play
The Vixen had 'gone a gathering'
It was not tired for had slept all day
Back and forth it paced frustrated
For to play required two
It was one and roots don't count
"To find a friend is what I must do"

So out of the Den it did venture
Out into a moonlit night
Employed the skills it had been taught
Move with caution and out of sight
Shortly it came across a Badger cub
Then saw others not far away
"Can I join you for some fun?"
"You are vermin we do not wish to play"

Saddened and startled the Fox cub retreated
"What have I done to cause that reaction?"
"What is vermin, my family name?"
"Why the hatred to my attraction?"
Fox cub next met a young bright Weasel
"Can I join you for play I must"
The Weasel looked at it and looked away
"No for you are sly and I do not trust"

Again rebuffed Fox cub continued
"What is wrong with what sly brings?"
Vixen told it was a talent
Nurture and your stomach sings
All night the cub encountered beings
Same request denied each time
So dejected as the dawn it broke
Returned to Den as if a crime
The moral of this little tale
Is not of hate or alarm
Just illustration of a victim
When reputation can cause you harm

A TOAST TO TANTRIC TUMBLES

Put my left leg here, right elbow there
Are you sure we've got this right
Your knee is digging in my kidneys
I'm know suffering from blurred sight
My left hand there, your right hand here
How do we hit Jackpot
With bodies twisted just as listed
We're copulating in a knot
I can't perceive how we're to breath
Yet alone achieve orgasm
When huff and puff at this strange stuff
We're Octopi just having spasm
I think my Back just popped a disc
For I was foolish and tried to kiss
Just as you did do figure thirty two
Known as a pelvic twist
Let's admit defeat while still complete
I like my body whole
We'll find new ways to make your eyes glaze
Without wriggling like Tadpole

Long gone those days of wild and crazed
When give anything a go
The aches and sprains and muscle strains
When try something didn't know
A Toast to Tantric tumbles
I still suffer from its rumbles
If can do then good for you
My attempt was full of stumbles

BAD DAY (MELEE OF THE MORNING MEAL)

I knew at once would be bad day
When entered Kitchen into foray
The Coffee and Toast had started a fight
The mood had simmered throughout the night
The Creamer and Butter had joined in
Two plus two can make a din
Teaspoon and knife just began to laugh
Plate and cup made circle path
Sugar and Jam I'd kept apart
In separate cupboards from the start

When Breakfast fights it's for the best
To go back to bed for some more rest
Hope it calms down before your lunch
Trust in hope and what's your hunch
Imagine my poor Kitchen
If this Breakfast had been cooked
Eggs and Bacon plaything Tag Team
Tea and Juice not overlooked
'Back to bed' that is my answer
Later clear the casualties, come what may
Mop, broom, bucket, the sibling saviours
When you wake up on bad day

BILLY THE BANJO

Five kids in town were feeling down
You know how the old story goes
Bland radio pop, no record shop
Nonexistent music shows
Five country kids with boots and lids
Skipping stones in Potters Creek
With yawns did spawn a dancing storm
To change things they did seek

'Let's make a Band by our own hands
Like those they have in Harrisberg
With our wills and some family skills
We'll be like none they've ever heard
Billy Town can win the crown
At The Folk Fest every year
We'll start off small until they call
We're musicians with no fear'

Maddie made a Mandolin
Gus did make Guitar
Desmond drummed while Hannah's Harmonica hummed
Stella sang like star
Billy the Banjo they called themselves
No reason for the name
Just came to them that day when
Their wish became the same

No genre they as they did play
Just made up as went
But when beat kicked in and Stella sings
A catchy message sent
Their rise it was historic, some say meteoric

Billboard charts did post their name, TV
shows tried to tap their fame
The world they travelled but their joy unravelled
They would never be the same

They did impress and then came stress
Those kids did strike true Gold
Went on for years but then the tears
As each their story told
The friendship turned to business
Business turned to friction
To keep top spot must give your lot
A dream became addiction

Maddie maddened at Mandolin
Gus gave up Guitar
Desmond dropped the drumming; Hannah's
Harmonica stopped its humming
Stella's singing sailed the stars
Billy the Banjo was a Band
A Band that hit the top
Just five kids with boots and lids
Who did not know to stop?

Recently I saw a tribute act
My sadness grew for their tale I knew
Of kids made good with strings and wood
But lost what's true as pressures flew
The kids turned adult, as they should
Within a place not understood
All said what they did was for their good
While milking the Brother and Sisterhood

CARNIVALS AND CELEBRATIONS

Carnivals and Celebrations
Festivals and salutations
Differ widely throughout the nations
Each does have their own fixations

Imagine if all honoured all
With the holidays for each one
Many days of colour and pageantry
Not many days to get things done

Forget just what we practice
On others religious days
Let them become a Faith friendly zone
Let's just see how that one plays

Think of the education
About how others choose to live
The fasting and the discipline
The joy when we do give

Geography in different plane
Philosophy as a new game
Deep inside we're all the same
Doing likewise in different name

Carnivals and Celebrations
Let's make them the new sensations
Do our bit to improve relations
Change the course of generations

PUZZLE PIECES

People are a mix of feelings
Sometimes they get it wrong
There is no blame in simple error
Just not the place that they belong

We explored and were found wanting
Sad it was but no-one's fault
Just two people in different worlds
They did try but bond was nought

So do not question and do not worry
None should ever take the blame
We are but pieces in a jigsaw
We just couldn't play that game

I never said that I love you
I never said that I'd try
Never promised you a Paradise
Is that the reason you said Good Bye?

A 'RICH KIDS' STORY

The child it sits on a staircase
For parents have no time to play
Nothing changes, it is so usual
Another disappointment for another day

Was like yesterday and those days before
Every day it is the same
Small talk at mealtimes before a phone rings
A frantic discussion and then away

Yes child knows they are lucky
For have all the toys a child could dream
None of that makes a difference
When in play they need a team

Lonely in their 'perfect world'
An upbringing perfect from outside
But only for adults who don't see the child
Only to them that their sadness they hide

Money is not so important
When alone when you are young
All the treasures in the world
Are based on love and having fun

CAME A VIRGIN

Came to town did a stranger
When I was younger and innocent
Had a look of someone different
Struck a statement where they went

Adults looked and changed direction
Every kid did wonder why
Parting seas just like in scriptures
Heads did lower as passed by

In the Square he chose to sit
Guess was weary and feeling tired
Yet something about him, maybe persona
Took my attention – I admired

Slowly approached for was uncertain
Feeling cautious with knees weak
Smiled at me when asked why was here
Took a sigh and they did speak

"We look at things with starry eyes
Then are filled with mild surprise
We think we know but we're blind
To the wishes of other kind
They're like us but are not
Maybe changed because what they've got
Still are dangerous to you and I
They just wish to know we die
That flash of light was of that bright
The boom that followed, can't describe
The scene before me I will not tell of
The picture type from which you hide

Came a Virgin - left a Man
Time so static and then it ran
Things I saw not known before
Hardship's a journey that needs a plan
I have seen Brothers and Sisters of different tone
That were Family that I call own
Give and fall then carry on
Then I look around to match their strong
Not all are made in their build
To common sense I've learned to yield
But not the look and not that stare
That, when return, they pretend to care
I'm just moving through to someplace new
One day a good one will I find too
Filled not with egos that needs salvation
Filled with souls that are my generation"

I walked back Home but journey lost me
Stunned by things that I did learn
Of people giving and sacrificing
So my freedom I could spurn

I made a move to make things different
Tried to make a wrong a right
Made a banner big and coloured
Made it large and made it bright

Not a lot that much was obvious
But a statement with what had
Until the age I could join that Family
Kept me straight and kept it glad

HIS PROMISE KEPT
Pagan – Conventional – Radical

On cobbled street tapped studded soles
Laces strung from shins to feet
Hem now ragged, slightly bloodstained
As to his Mother he went to meet
Shield on back and sword in scabbard
Spear swaying slowly in his hand
Had been and gone, one of brothers
Now he walked on home soil land
He made a promise – more an oath
To his Mother as she said and wept
"Return with your shield or on upon it"

He now returned with promise kept
He'd stood bare armed with just bronze lower arm guard
Shoulder to shoulder with those like him
Social bonding within his training
Made another kith and kin
Helmet sweaty upon his forehead
Leather strap biting beneath his chin
Dust sore eyes gazed somewhat weary
To see from where this did begin
Trying to erase those sounds of anger
Blown out loud from orders horn
Then the malaise – blurred and frantic
The call of arms to which was born

Mother cried when she did meet him
Of relief for different things
He was back and carried shield
No vicious murmur and what that brings
Duty is a heavy burden

When expectations run so high
Born and brainwashed, no surrender
Fight and live or fight and die

Forward on almost two millennia
Different battle but same thought
'Death before Dishonour' rings out loudly
New weapons feature, same battle fought
Now the pressure is so much greater
For have learned from some mistakes
Yet the blinkered run his army
One stubborn fool is all that takes
This time opponents can kill from distance
Using tools Spartan never dreamed
Gone is shield, now a foxhole
Strewn in metals we have gleaned
No more a shield to one carries
Now consists of mass made cask
Yet still demanding those he's leaving
To hurry up and complete his task
Media now do live reporting
Both sides watch and listen for a clue
Analysis comes from those whom shut out
Fight own battle for something new

The modern soldier fought outnumbered
Saw a truth that did not please
Dropped his weapons and surrendered
Hoped and prayed for quick release
Had been trained in 'surviving capture'
Knew the tricks and what was new
Survive to fight another day
His promise kept and thus would do

Now forward again a few more decades
For the soldier creed has changed again
Gone is enemy on the battlefield
Now non-combatants are fair game
The code of conduct has reverted
Past the Trojan and beyond
Now the rules are set by psychos
Of just hurting others they are fond
Their call to arms is just a splinter
Radicals within religion
Brainwashed seekers of invisible riches
Though of that faith is just a smidgeon
Terrorist and round the twist
Somehow match hand in hand
Honour grown and honour shown
Somehow seem a mythical land

That one time searcher for their questions answer
Became a tool of others dreams
They play games but from a distance
Not really believing so it seems
The 'soldier' stood with no glory
Other than what's in his head
Kept his promise that will not be honoured
He just died a toy instead

When cause is needed for an action
Though you can't make a true decision
Play the one that can be perverted
Stoke the fires called religion
We've fought each other and our own
Sometimes same faith with different views
Radicals take to next level
An excuse to make the news
All soldiers fight with their Gods behind them

Sometimes invoke in time of fear
Though enemies are those that fight them
Not the families and those held dear

Pagan, Conventional, Radical
Charts the warrior through the ages
Two had codes if somewhat complex
Third has none but fills our pages
Quick to enter, quick forgotten
Without honour just pure rage
Impact now but soon condemned them
Just new terrorist of a new age

CHORAL CHANT OF THE MODEM MASSES

One posted on a social bed
Others comment what's in their head
Builds in number and tempo
Said out loud so all do know
One types a line another follows
Covers all and everything, all the joys and all the sorrows
Diversity bridges our impasses
Choral chant of the Modem masses
So many subjects, so many voices
We all partake and all rejoices
To be one of many a comfort spread
None do lead and none are led

When cold wind blows
The circles in our lake
Distant Drums roll like Thunder
Loneliness is the coldest Home
When the clock strikes midnight
I walk a familiar path
When you were mine so long ago
I paint a picture of my life

So many lines of random statement
Knit together seamlessly
Many characters joined together
As though I was you and you were me

A single letter becomes a word
A word becomes a line
Some spelt different for that is beauty
When nations write the work's divine

Tapestries are woven, pictures painted
So now I am hooked and time it passes
When caught up and sucked in
Choral chant of the modem masses

TODAY I DREAM OF AVALON

Of steeded knights and things to come
The beauty in a purpose true
The quest that ends when I have you
Round Table for we have no edges
Knights of old who kept their pledges
A quest secured and moves along
To build together new Avalon

The man he saddled and urged his steed
Though to find the answer he had no need
Just the quest that deep did burn
The gift of love he'd someday learn
A noble though not of old meaning
Still same yearning and want leaning
So set forth did new Knight
To venture through the day and night
There would be Dragons and Temptress too
For did venture in land so new
Of words and pictures but no being
Of 'character' but no seeing
He bears a shield of Understanding;
Sword of being what is shown
Emblem that of acceptance, armour the comfort of being own

Today I dream of Avalon
Of steeded knights and things to come
The beauty in a purpose true
The quest that ends when I have you
Round Table for we have no edges
Knights of old who kept their pledges
A quest secured and moves along
To build together new Avalon

The Damsel too had a story
One she thought and chose to hide
Not of disgrace or embarrassment
For she had virtue and she had pride
Two troubled souls that not seeking
Unbeknown were just planned
He ventured out with no clear purpose
She saw his soul and gave her Hand
His Oath he swore, she gave her favour
He pledged his life and she did savour
The modern Knight and Lady fair
We now be because we dare

The Camelot though stuff of fable
Can resurrect for we are able
Our quest has ended and just begun
For together we build our Avalon

THE DESERT OF LIFE

I trekked across that barren Desert
Soul determined and full of pride
For had a vision of what awaited
The surge of joy I could not hide
Over sands that were so lonely
One step further and one step nearer
Sun bears down and Mirage rises
Through it all is sight so clear
An Oasis comes and with it strangers
Fellow travellers upon their quest
There took time and paused a while
There did I lay head to rest
Morning came so on I journeyed
Ever further into new me
Am progressing in my fulfilment
Closing on what's meant to be
The path of life is a solemn one
Not for those so full of doubt
You cross a Desert to your paradise
Though you must believe and carry out
Questions came and questions went
Though not until I answered true
For situations were the questions
Every experience it held a clue

AMAZON ECHOES

The notes did float as he did play
Body perked and began to sway
Behind my eyes I saw a scene
Of a place I have not been

Forested lands and creatures hid
Watercolours and humid
Indigenous tribes naively pure
Unaware of the illness and our cure

Music simple and music straight
From a land that seems so great
Haunting, stirring, captivating
So removed from our love of hating

Some parts now a tourist scene
Some for harvest or have been
Still the mystery stays with me
Of the parts that we can't see

From the depths of the unknown
To the High street that has grown
Amazon Echoes resonate
Has me hoping this is not its fate

Somewhere on this modern land
Should be a Temple unscarred by man
If only just so can remind
Natures glory if we are kind

Baked this morning

Cottage Loaf, Bloomer too
Deep fried Donuts and pastries Choux
Split tin Loaf, Crusty Batons
Multitudes just for you

Baba bread and Ajdov Kruh
Apple bread, Banana too
Viennese Whirls, white iced Fingers
Caramel shortcake is something new

BAKED THIS MORNING

Gone by noon
More in oven
Coming soon

Flat bread, Pitta bread, choice of Naans
Soft roll, Crusty roll, Finger roll, Bap
Jam tart, Treacle tart, Custard's good
Belgian Bun, Bakewell slice, Beverage on tap

Soda bread, Brown bread, Fruit loaf too
Brioche, Ciabatta, Panattone
Egg tart, Apple pie, cherry sweet
Swiss roll, Chocolate roll, Bruttiboni

Baked this morning
Gone by noon
More in oven
Coming soon

Next Batch please!
What you want
Not on list?
Give us the recipe
We'll make your wish

Business is new and looking good
We are raring, we are keen
Seeing products simply flying
Is the stuff of long time dream?

BEHIND SAD EYES

Behind sad eyes she looks at me
I don't even know her name
She smiles a smile of forced happiness
Brushed aside the pain the same

And when night comes the tears flow freely
Wash away the hurt once more
And in the night the mask it slips
When chill and worry come to the fore
Never was this supposed to happen
Waste of birth to die each day
When your world is now so muted
Because you know not what to say

Behind the hand so gently trembling
Stands a body worn and frail
Dirty clothes on washed torso
Arms and legs tell their own tale

And when night comes a new dwelling
Just some sleep is her deepest wish
Counts the coins she has collected
Too soft the rattles in her tin dish
Nothing worth waking for tomorrow
Except belief that it will change
Those with plenty seem unhappy
To those with nothing it seems so strange

I see this girl nearly always
Still same place and still same smile
I empty pocket to fill dish and stomach
If not forever then for a while

And when day comes that she has gone
In her place stands someone new
Will she have left a parting message?
Just a hint or just a clue?
All of us in some strange way
Carry on but don't realise
Sometimes behind the sweetest smile
A story lies behind sad eyes

CUPID, MARS AND APHRODITE

Billy sat chewing the fat
With his group of mates
Acting cool for was his rule
Beside his old school gates

Mary sat in classroom
Gazed through the window pane
Looked in awe at what she adored
Billy was his name

Cupid shot his arrow
Mars did use his shield
Aphrodite then she got tough
Young Billy had to yield
When those hormones lead
The body does follow
Piece by piece, bit by bit
Billy found his pride did swallow

Billy knew Mary for they were neighbours
Though of her feelings he was a stranger
Acting tough and being cool
Had no idea his mask would fall

Then one day quite by chance
The local club it held a dance
Mary and friends they went along
There was Billy acting strong

As the songs did come and songs did go
He asked girls to dance but they didn't want to know
Then saw Mary by the wall alone
To Billy was a dog with bone

"Hi there Mary! How are you?
Shall we show these fools that have no clue
It just so happens quite by chance
Before you is a man that can dance"

Mary smiled and then did laugh
"Should I ask for an autograph?
Only joking, come let's go
Sounds like time this world should know"

Cupid shot his arrow
Mars did use his shield
Aphrodite then she got tough
Young Billy had to yield
When those hormones lead
The body does follow
Piece by piece, bit by bit
Billy found his pride did swallow

Now Billy and Mary are a couple
She makes him happy and keeps out of trouble
He shows her a side that few knew
When true love strikes you have no clue

"ELLO MISTER"

'Ello Mister, spare a copper?
'Ello Mister, you seen the Light?
'Ello Mister, you look learned
'Ello Mister, help my plight
'Ello Mister, you be right dapper
'Ello Mister, you look alright
'Ello Mister, I say it true
'Ello Mister, bet you have might
'Ello Mister, alright is you
'Ello Mister, I got no-one
'Ello Mister, don't know me Dad
'Ello Mister, me mums a drunkard
'Ello Mister makes me right sad
'Ello Mister, spare a penny
'Ello Mister, you know you wanna
'Ello Mister, for is charity
'Ello Mister, else I'm a goner
'ELLO MISTER, don't turn your back!
'Ello Mister, ignores is cruel
'Ello Mister, I 'ave me dreams
'Ello Mister, don't play the fool
Hello Mister, you are a disgrace sir
Hello Mister, your stench is foul
Hello Mister, you offend me
Hello Mister, be gone now!

ASPIRATIONS TAKE HIATUS

Teacher stood in front of class
Had been speaking of Hopes and Dreams
Students had answered in the negative
Said real life was not as seems

Teacher knew what they were feeling
Had taught this age for many years
The transition of instant to that of waiting
Created turmoil and failures fears

Stood still a while to gain attention
Breathed in deep and lifted head
Began a recital spoken often
Gazed at Students and then said

"Let aspirations take hiatus
Never let them fade away
They will come to fore and flourish
Maybe next year if not today

The biggest test that you'll encounter
Will not be set by likes of me
I just set a strong foundation
For you to build what want to be

When you leave here and do scatter
On different journeys - each your own
Tests of conviction will stand before you
They will make you feel alone

Each test is personal though many will sit it
Designed by Fate and Destiny
Everyone has their own future
This test is for you personally

Patience and commitment are its answer
Then your aspirations can evolve
Take hiatus in pursuing reckless
When time is right you will resolve

Many a Student has passed through my lessons
Many now have achieved their Dream
Sometimes sitting back is moving forwards
Hopefully one day you'll see what mean

Turn todays disappointed into tomorrows joyful
Just by not rushing blindly in
Rejection is fuel that can move you upwards
So from today you should begin

Failure is just little steps
That tell you not Today
Perhaps tomorrow if you're willing
Will call again and maybe play

The determined wear like Badges
Every knock back they have had
Tell the world made more determined
Never let it make them sad

Inside each of you is a fire
Burning brightly but not yet seen
Sometimes winds blow and almost extinguish
But flames roar back for are your Dream"

CEDRIC SNOWMAN

Cedric Snowman went to Jail
For poor Frosty did impale
With a carrot hard and cold
This the story that he told

"Officer, Officer, Officer please
I did not mean it! I just sneezed!
Frosty was showing me his good luck charm
But I've got a cold - I meant no harm

It just flew off in his direction
To cause him death had no intention
Officer please you must believe me
The put pointy end out when did build me

I cannot go to jail oh no
In there I'll melt! No-one will know
Become a puddle on the floor
Then of Cedric there'll be no more"

The Officer took note of what he heard
To the Custody Sergeant did have word
The sergeant was a clever geezer
He turned a cell into a freezer

There he stayed for just two days
Outside his cell a moisture haze
There was no case for you see
When Sun came out Frosty ceased to be

BUBBLING BROOK

Bubbling Brook why this course you took?
To get to who knows where
You weave and turn to your efforts earn
A mass that doesn't care
Takes you in amongst the other things
Feeds are what it yearns
Gets a name and tourists fame
Yet you they seem to spurn
One stretch fast but cannot last
Your course it does dictate
Depth of bed, spread overhead
Must leave you most irate

You are sedation – my meditation
Whenever visit you
Get lost in time and that's just fine
When of present have no clue
Bubbling Brook to you I look
For example of invention
You parch and go then show and flow
A classic rebirth worth a mention
Of rocks and shale when dry so pale
You give a polish sheer
Of limbs and things heat dullness brings
You place a bright veneer

THE CANDID KID

Spent some time down a Mine
Way down in the South
Work was hard but life was harder
Existing hand to mouth

Worked and scraped, scraped and worked
Earned enough to settle down
Not here with all the wannabes
I chose a quiet Town

Met someone and settled down
Together had a kid
Raised them proper and taught respect
Though a secret we both hid

Now wed eighteen with girl seventeen
The past has come again
Like a blast from my past
The story starts and penned

The candid Kid came calling
In stutter he did tell
He'd summed up all his courage
To seek time with his belle

The Father watched as Mother welcomed
He had played that game
Nervousness but prospective bliss
Once he was the same

Dad moved to corner full of shadow
So none could see his smile
'Shyness you old Rooster
You've been gone awhile'

The candid Kid delivered lines
The Mothers heart did melt
I stood with pride although did hide
His words that I'd spelt

Words tuned down to lessen frown
A Rooster has his time
Though to settle must soften mettle
Then will find his prime

AND I REMEMBERED

Alas poor souls I felt your are hurting
My dreams and hopes were torn asunder
You breathed into me a strange sensation
You spoke not of calm but sound of thunder

Hope the sister of Despair
You two played me like a game of Dice
I throw a six and I am winning
Throw two Ones and I lose twice

Once before you did haunt and taunt
But oh so well I know you now
You raise up - then slam down
You offer hope then destroy - and how!

Sweet, so sweet the dreams offered me
Those implanted firmly within my Head
With a smile you created ambition
Though I have memory so enough said

Irony and false expectation
I bewildered with no distinction
All I saw was just confusion
But I remember another reason

And I remember our games before
I do know you can be beaten
I remember the price of winning
Remember Humble Pie that I have eaten

And I remember the cold of loneliness
I remember the warmth of friends
I remember the start of journeys
I remember journey's end

And I remember the bitter taste of sadness
Remember the sweetness of first joy
I remember the first female kisses
I remember first punch of a Boy

Remember too my first day of working
I remember feeling so out of touch
I remember getting first pay check
And I remember was not very much

I remember my first try at writing
And I remember wanting to be
I remember reading other's poems
I remember Poets like me

DRIVE

The night slips by with the distance
So drive my friend, just drive
A day of bliss is my objective
Drive on friend, just drive

Working week tensions drain with daydreams
Slip further through a rear view mirror
As the landscape flashes by
So reality seems so much clearer

This journey is such smooth sweet calm
The wheels spin just like my day
Memories like fleeting objects
The destination is always play

For road signs warn of impending danger
You are for-armed when for-warned
Have time to prepare and brace yourself
When as life you hit a storm

Smooth and steady is a perfect journey
A to B with no deviation
No distraction when seeking pleasure
Vehicle just rolls without variation

Distance is the perfect barrier
Drive on my friend, just drive
Look towards and not backwards
Drive on please, just drive

ACCENT THE ASPIRING ACTIONS

The boy he sat with his Father's Father
Gazing up at favourite wall
Upon which told of man bold
Much younger then and tall

A portrait of a successful man
With awards hung either side
That they were for acts of sharing
Filled the young boy with such pride

'This is how I want to be'
Said the boy inside his head
'This is how to be remembered
This a tribute to life led'

"Grandpa, how did you find the courage
To decide to do what did?
To stand up and face the hardships
While most others hid"

The old man turned to answer question
A warm smile shone on face
"Son, first you must find something inside you
It is beautiful and called Grace"

"I know of Grace and try to have it"
Replied the boy with answer true
"But what then drives one to achieve things
Achievements such as those to you"
"Well lad, let me see"
Said the man placing hand on shoulder
"Learn this lesson young
Don't wait until you're older

First you must believe yourself
Before you ask others to believe in you
Not the belief that you can trick them
But the belief that it is true
Confidence is providence
For a journey that lies ahead
Yourself can grow with seeds you sow
The choice of path you tread
Accent the aspiring actions
Pure intent needs no retractions
Each level raising nearer goal
To have virtues makes kind soul
Never lambaste but encourage
For harsh words only do discourage
Warn of pitfalls if there's potential
If you share there's no confidential
Be the person of your Dreams
There's no barrier as stout as seems
Most importantly always walk tall
For Snakes do slither and they can't call"

With that said the old man joined the boy
Gazing at that wall
"One day your portrait will hang here
For I can see you're no-one's fool"

CHANGED THE RIVER

Man he changed the River
From where it used to flow
Dug and damned with own hand
To plant seed and then grow

Man did harness Wind with sail
To both travel and to grind
Inventiveness was the test
Solutions he did find

Man invented a circular thing
Then he called it Wheel
Easier over land to travel
With suspension it had less feel

Man he changed the lie of land
For Homes that could then build
Creating concrete jungle spots
From what he had made as field

Man he built the Aeroplane
To help us keep in touch
Shortened time it took to travel
To those we miss so much

Man he changed the River
So can change what feel inside
Change for future better
By losing foolish pride

TRI COLOUR MERGE

Reaction, Emotions, Danger show
Sometimes a stranger of friend I know
Too complicated an anagram heard
For what is just a three letter word
We see it when our blood a blazing
See it when our sense a fazing
We sense it when we think of danger
When signs put up by a stranger
R.E.D. So much more
When use of colour we explore
Long time nature painted loud
I am wearing so not allowed
Vibrant, vivid, catches eye
Yet signals reward or do not try
A puzzle in significance
A sign to bar or recompense

Blue the colour of our sky
At least as seen by human eye
Tranquil, calming if we try
The colour of things now gone by

The Sea is Blue as often written
The Sea in fact can be grey or green
But Blue suggests calm and tranquil
Others hide a darker scene

When sad and thoughtful we are Blue
When cold to terminal we turn Blue
When friendly casualties Blue on Blue
When style of music called the Blues

Blue so opposite from the Red
Conflicting shades within the Head
Though can merge in palette bed
Become a new and join instead

Purple

Red the fire of passion found
Blue the feel of something lost
Give and take in equal measures
Purple the gain, purple the cost

Nothing bitter, no revenge
Nothing much to avenge
Serenity is a Heart in flower
Hope eternal with purple power

What was found and what was lost
They are subjects none can see
They are personal, individual
They are part of being ME

A welcome colour for is so warming
Full of richness yet full of somehow meek
Vibrant, deep, encapsulating
Describes the life we wish to seek

THE FAMILY OF MOTHER LIFE

Father Time and Mother Life
Once wed in a land unheard
They had a family of many children
Each was named a four letter word

Love was a daughter oh so varied
Hate a son so full of fire
Hope, she was an optimist
Pain, he fought cousin Desire
Envy did have a spiteful soul
Lust had a friend called Greed
Want was confused and never clear
Need did endeavour and succeed
Meet was one half of twins
Part was twin of Meet
Open (heart) was generous
Shut hated chance to greet
Give had a friend called Sharing
Lose was nicknamed Spurned
Stay was dogged and persistent
Gone was reflective when had learned

As is always with a family
They did fight and they did share
Father Time and Mother Nature
Also had a girl called Care

BORN INSIDE YOU

I came from Forest deep and ancient
Yet in the present I am near
I manifest within the thinking
My modern name? They call me Fear

I came from the skies when you looked up
When you fell deep I gave strength to cope
I am all things and ever present
Have many names but I am Hope

I come from parents Failure and Hurting
I am abomination bright and pure
Find my victims then exploit them
To you am known as Insecure

I am what you created
You met Hope and thus whence
Made a child for Hope to nurture
You made me – Confidence

In a Human I was created
Counter Doubt as you must
I am the nemesis of Insecure
I am Hopes cousin, I am Trust

You have us all deep within you
All of us and many more
It is you that can find and choose us
But to find you must explore

PEGASUS

We all hope and dream
Will or future seem
A fitting story on our page
Of purpose achieved
Of loved one grieved
From adolescence until old age

The rush of blood in stolen kiss
Ache so deep of those we miss
Transcending all words that can describe them true
The thrill of ambition
Hurts rendition
The thoughts of me and you

Everyone needs a sun
An object to throw warm glow
Upon a future thought
The bright and light
Give light at night
In Ether love is caught

On Pegasus we fit the saddle
Adjust the bridle and grip the reins
Feet in stirrups and kick the heels
Ride the rush of layered plains

Drive on you beast of noble virtue
Dig deep your hooves in hidden soil
Thrust with intent your feathered wings
Show us the joy within toil

You beat, you bet, you noble beast
We do seek each everyone
The chance to run and then fly
To find the person we will become
We seek the help and you provide
An inspiration to focus sight
When believe, we will fight
No stretch to far, no gap too wide

SIMPLE

Simple are the dreams of Humans
Simple is a 'perfect world'
Simple is the lust for Life
Simple is a voice not heard

Simple is your desire
Simple is to carry on
Simple is a choice to make
Simple is where we belong

Simple are these words of wisdom
Simple are a friends advice
Simple is an understanding
Simple is a past so wise

Simple is that thing called 'Love'
Simple is when it is shared
Simple is the eternal journey
Simple when two have cared

Simple is not understanding
Simple is for getting wrong
Simple is for living dreams
Simple is when don't belong

Simple is just progression
Simple is the brand new day
Simple is others thoughts
Simple is when they do say

RAISE MY GLASS

The man he sat one September day
Home and Family far away
On the anniversary of his birth
Picked up a pen and with it say

'It's my Birthday and I'll laugh if I want to
For alone but with Family and friends
Gone is the need for face to face with
With technology and modern trends

Current time is now unimportant
Someone is up somewhere out there
Hit a button and you're connected
To share a joke or view to air

Speak to loved ones far away
Just right now are deeply missed
Though get comfort with their vision
Tastes quite different when screen kissed

I am alone but never lonely
I am content amongst loved and friends
I thank the creator of the microchip
I pray this trend never ends

It's my Birthday and I'll smile if I want to
The journey's good along life's street
So I raise my glass and make a toast
To Loved and Friends, present and those to meet'

The moral of this verse is
Happiness is just a state
State of Mind I'll think you'll find
One of many you can create

———

BEFORE TOO OLD

Spent my summer travelling
Finding out things new
My winter working at odd jobs
To pay for what could do
Packed light for ease of travel
Had heard the stories told
Took my chance to live a different life
Before I got too old

Camel ride in Egypt
Ostrich race in Oz
Tried rafting down the Tongariro
Saw the history shown at Kos
Eaten a Banana cue in the Philippines
Served expats in Hong Kong
Unlike me they'd settled down
They knew where did belong

I learnt Customs has so many meanings
Economy just the same
It's amazing how you view the world
When play the Traveller Game
Returned with Passport filled with many stamps
Memories hot and cold
So glad I lived a different life
Before I got too old

A START

Did someone say a song that plays
Sends a message to the heart
Well I guess my friend that in the end
At least that is a start

Did we begun as two and then we grew
Three became a one
We rearranged and our lives changed
When families do what's done

When we grieve to stress relieve
Doesn't mean that we don't care
About those that left and also bereft
Of one no longer there

Did you read and then perceive
A writer exploring human action
If you did thank you I did
For using of your time a fraction

To look at what another writes
While passing quiet time
So do it well in Prose too tell
I just prefer to rhyme

CELESTE

Celeste she was a Wood Nymph
She liked to play within the Trees
Had conversations with the Caterpillars
Played Chase Me with the Bees

Celeste she had four main jobs
I guess they were her reason
Different roles at different times
When her Boss did change the Season

In the springtime was to encourage
The buds and the new born
Help them grow so they could show
The radiance they will adorn

Summer was presentation
Teach them how to use the light
To boldly show so all could know
A future pure and bright

Autumn she taught them giving
How for blessings they should pay
Give back some but keep some back
For then they could still stay

Winter was the hardest task
For to clean her House again
Decisions made, sometimes afraid
She couldn't hide her pain

Celeste she has been around for ages
She couldn't tell her age
For cycle was forever
Four Seasons make one page

———

TO CREATE A PERSON
(Please refer to diagram included)

Take a head and insert a brain
Take a torso and add in a heart
Attach the face and give it eyes
Now can see, think and even love – at least that's a start
Now take the body and give it arms
Then to their ends attach the hands
At the bottom of torso fix two strong legs
Attach feet to travel life's slippery sands

On face fix nose to breathe and smell
Create a mouth including the tongue
Alongside heart insert two strong lungs
To provide power when rapture sung
To whole run veins and fill with blood
To feed the muscles we all need
Encase with pigment shaded cover skin
To help define their kin and creed

Now we truly are onto something
Add soul to work with heart
Link these to combine with brain
Now will get conscience and will to start
Activate in brain switch marked Memory
So mistakes are not repeated
Engage 'Opinion and sense of right'
To ensure your creation is not cheated

Thread in nerves to sense warning signs
Give ears on head to hear sound
In mouth place teeth to help them eat
Switch on 'Balance' to help around

Place the other included organs
Within your being before you forget
To help convert food for fuel
And control temperature by sweat

To stop this being getting cold
Attach hair to the stated parts
Though this is sometimes unwanted
Can be removed and set apart
Locate in brain switch called 'Style'
Check it is set to 'random choice'
Place in throat item marked larynx
To give your person thing called voice

Place reproductive organs where stated
Of which sex you can now decide
Switch on 'desire' for thing called fashion
So these organs we can hide
Now let's get really creative
And insert a sense of humour
Add ability to reject or doubt
And imagination to prevent stupor

Install extra muscles around the mouth
To let them make a smile
Give coughing bursts of thing called laughter
Though for safety sake restrict its length and style
Add quirks and individuality
Of your personal choice
Behold! You have created your own person
In your achievements you can now rejoice!

(No refunds available)

MYSTERY BLUE

Mystery Blue was her name
Racing others was her game
With long strides did target chase
Sleek and slim and with such grace

She was a showgirl so well known
Privileged was one that own
Had the best of everything
So rewards she could then bring

In her prime she had no equal
Long gone now her finest days
Yet still people talk of her
Her achievements logged and stays

Saw Mystery Blue once or twice
On TV in the News
Never met her personally
For her game I didn't choose

Still admired what she did
As she sped like speed of sound
Around the track imperiously
Mystery Blue was a fine Greyhound

A Greyhound like of which has never been
A Greyhound that before not seen
Covered track like an Exocet
Firm hot favourite of those who bet

I wonder where she is now.
For is old and racing over
I hope she's enjoying retirement
Chasing Rabbits in fields of clover

CLEANSING

The aroma of crushed Mint Leaf
The menthol slicing through
Damp chill upon a Meadow
Supplied by morning Dew

The shower after exercise
Dry clothes you then adorn
First cry after labour
As new life is born

The crispness of fresh water
On the throat so parched
The feel of ironed collar
When it is washed and starched

The slight saltiness of Ocean
As comes visiting on the shore
Leaving little presents
Before withdrawn back once more

The confession of an error
That's been nagging for a while
Wave of relief when get no grief
Just the knowing smile

Completing act of worship
For those of religious leaning
Cleansing has so many ways
Not just a soul had cleaning

To be cleansed in different ways
Is the product of the caring
Taking gifts that some do miss
Yet are for the sharing

I find cleansing in my penning words
De-cluttering random thought
Maybe not the most entertaining works
For the penner is self taught

Yet the reason's not important
When feel fresher I do find
Scrawling things as I think
Verse of Idle Mind

To pen can be so cleansing
To read is cleansing too
Share what I think with use of ink
You can cleanse me too

THE DARK

We face the dark in our deepest hours
We welcome the dark when want to hide
We look at the dark when are doubting
We talk to the dark when lose our guide

All have doubts and all have pain
All carry scars that were hard earned
All had hopes so cruelly shattered
All have lessons harshly learned

We consider the dark as an option
The darkness of losing care
We touch the dark in desperation
We welcome dark when no-one's there

So shun the dark and find a friend
So avoid the dark and realise
We fight the dark with the light
We beat the dark because we are wise

THE FAMILY

Thud went my sense of reality
Boom went the dream as truth kicked in
Hiss went my breath as I exhaled
Silence came as thought 'where to begin?'

Another knockback in a world of knockbacks
Cousins Rejection with partner Fail
The black sheep of the achievement family
For they do not believe to chase the Grail

I've met that family so many times
All the relatives some more than others
All hide their names behind your achievements
They do lurk as life we uncover

I do not avoid them nor try to hide
For they will find you all the same
I just choose to which I listen
This will help me achieve my aim

I like the sisters Hope and Courage
They are positive with a spark
Also Thoughtful and Determined
I like the message they do hark

The Family of our experience
A random family to be sure
Led by Wish and Opportunity
They do love to knock on a door

The art is just to stand back and listen
As they sell gusto and zeal
Sift the fact from the fiction
Concentrate on what could be real

This family are immortal
Go way back and will beyond
Grudgingly I admire them
In a secret way I am fond
For they are part of me inside
They do live in all with thought
Their constant duel to be the loudest
Have been a lesson so well taught

COME SUNDAY COME SLEEP DAY

The week's been long, now don't feel so strong
Give me please a Sunday
As week progresses so do my stresses
Where are you my Sunday
Sunday is my fun day
The day I get to choose
Can go out can laugh or shout
Can just stay in and snooze

How many hours are in this week?
Have they added but not told
Each time I wake seems just remake
A slower version of the old
Come Sunday that all changes
Come Sunday it rearranges
Come Sunday come my play day
Come Sunday come my sleep day

And on that day I will forget
If only for a week
I will not that day be bitter
Nor will I vengeance seek
The World can do its own thing
Just leave me quite alone
Then you will not be a target
As I rest on pillow throne

I am quite good natured
I tolerate six days of Hell
Sunday is my own day
It's when I break the spell
Come to me my Sunday
Hurry if you will
You alone keep me normal
Sunday the sanity pill

MIDNIGHT RISING

Came upon a place called Midnight
Quaint old place full of peace
All the pent up vim and anger
Stopped at boundary and did release

I've toured the jungles and then cities
Where the fury likes to hide
Crossed the waters, vast and open
Chased the idol we call pride

In the wilderness of my travels
Found this time and found this place
Gave up its first name and became Midnight
The first title Amazing Grace

Now I've settled in at Midnight
All is calm and peaceful here
Can again walk down the main road
Without worry, without fear

Nothing ventured nothing gain
Though, sometimes, must learn restrain
It takes one pull to take a life
Yet takes wisdom to get a Wife

Midnight rising over long grass
Midnight rising over sand
Midnight rising over waters
Midnight rising over land

CONSEQUENCES OF CONSCIOUS CONSCIENCE

The worker who went back to fix
Their mistake without being asked
The Paramedic that attended scene
Off duty so not tasked

The Teacher that buys the tools
So the students can still learn
The owner to create a Fire Break
Will watch their Home burn

The Driver who leaves their details
When they scrape a parked car
The friend that stuck beside you
When you went too far

The Child that extends the Olive Branch
Before the playground fight
The debater that admits defeat
When know the other person's right

The Samaritan who stops to ask
The person who looks distressed
Consequences of conscious conscience
In that they are all blessed

What makes the ones that do right?
Instead of walk away
What is the message that they hear
What exactly does it say?

I am not sure but I am glad
That someone hears those words
For if all were deaf we'd be at best
Conglomerates of unfeeling herds

We should make these people Leaders
In our Community and Town
Mock and jeer at those conceited
That moans about and frowns

The conscious conscience of consequences
A rare and treasured gift
Not all of us do own it
But all of us do lift

THE DREAM SPEAKS

I come to you to bring you peace
I travel from where you can't see
My route to you is restricted
My entrance when your thoughts are free

So many times I wait on borders
As you hover restless grim
Never sure my manifestations
For you decide what I will bring

I live outside you but you make me
Influenced by waking day
Can act random, sometimes crazy
I am just your brain at play

I am unique, never matching
Similar but not exact
Themes repeating with some changes
Funny how you make me act

When you are calm then I am happy
When you are troubled I'm troubled too
When adventurous I am eccentric
When you are searching I give a clue

When you wake I will vanish
May sometimes leave a memory hazy
Just short term for to confuse you
Real or not? I can make you crazy

I work best when eyes are closed
For only then complete attention
To run amok with all your senses
I am the child of your invention

———

L

O

V

E

BOUNCE, BOUNCE

Bounce, bounce goes the rubber ball
Bounce, bounce as the children rush
Bounce, bounce it goes off walls and pavement
Bounce, bounce the footsteps with faces flush

Bounce, bounce teenage emotions
Bounce, bounce the thoughts of the naive
Bounce, bounce the cost of growing older
Bounce, bounce the target to achieve

Bounce, bounce the finances we have in life
Bounce, bounce the cost of growing up
Bounce, bouncethe lessons taught to us
Bounce, bounce the contents of 'loving cup'

Bounce, bounce is being and creating
Bounce, bounce is the tempo of our life
Bounce, bounce is the chance when I ask you
Bounce, bounce the question 'will you be my wife?'

THE PRIZE

'The journey it has been long
The path it crumbled under me
The stamina it was threatened
The end so distant I could not see

But the goal was worth the effort
The achievement I could surmise
All forgotten and all forgiven
When I reached and took the Prize

It broke some dreams
It broke some bonds
It asked some questions I'd never thought
It created rights and created wrongs'

'Was it worth it?' 'Absolutely!'
'Have regrets?' 'Yes that's life!'
'Would you change anything?' 'Maybe with hindsight'
'What did you achieve?' 'I got the Prize!'

MINI YOU AND MINI ME

Mini you and mini me
Think of all the fun we'd see
For are not real just fantasy
Grown up imps that we could be

Life a blast of youthful frolic
Never drinking alcoholic
Just the joy of naughty dares
Run away with no guilty cares

Mini you and mini me
Part of mini family
Mini child upon your knee
Mini we are mini three

Mini Bus to mini Mart
We might be small but we'd be smart
Mini breaks at mini cost
Major ones would leave us lost

Mini bodies massive Heart
Major love each day start
Mini troubles much, much fun
All days happy when begun

Mini you and mini me
With mini Dog we'd call Fugi
What a picture we would be
If mini us we could be

LOVE ACROSS THE OCEANS

You wake up early and they stay up late
Just for the chance to talk
Exchange of words through ether or phone call
One day will happen when they can walk

To share a home as well as thoughts
To hold each other's hands
To show in solid what they described
When talked of distant land

Though of different shores and different cultures
Share a history within their past
Something sparked and something happened
Became a love that's meant to last

Lived each other's lives by the minute
Have joined in mutual trust
Met and moved to higher ground
Sidestepped that thing called Lust

They now plan for a future
With thought and care so true
To ensure a world of Harmony
They think like partners do

Though it is hard and filled with wanting
Sometimes dreams become a notion
Strong is love that will find a cure
For a love across the Oceans

TWO SHIPS

Across the sea of Serendipity
Sail two vessels within sight
Never meeting bur always greeting
We're two ships passing in the night

When you say morning in my afternoon
You do live so far away
We adapt to situations
Both understand what other say

We have that bond called Chemistry
Our souls are twinned in what we do
When you speak I do listen
Within your words I find the clue

Highs and lows we have shared them
Go around the world then meet again
We come together then sail away
Though keep in touch with use of pen

Maybe someday winds will calm
Then can float there side by side
Tied together and joined together
Then two ships on the ocean Pride

NUMBER ONE

So to sleep in foreign lands
Friends now choose to lay at rest
Though unseen are not forgotten
Barriers broken for the best

Today I woke and sought a friendship
Easy when they are worldwide
To listen in or speak out loud
You do chose or you do hide

Today was quiet though of choice
For today I listened in
Some interaction was impulsive
Some expression on a whim

Today was good for the right reasons
For today controlled what did come
Today was change of repetition
Today I felt number one

UTOPIA WITHIN YOUR KISS

You are the colours of the spectrum
You are the notes of a favourite song
You are the stars within my universe
Everywhere is where you belong

I breathe the air and smell your scent
I hear the wind and know your voice
I taste the nectar that you send me
All that I am is through your choice

I am a creation of your forming
I am a tool for your pleasure
Though I do not mind what my status
For what you take give in equal measure

Now I have purpose and I have need
I have found contentment and found bliss
For in a world of hate and confusion
I have found Utopia within your kiss

LODIETA MY SPECIAL ROSE

Lodieta dreams of happy things
Her thoughts are pure and true
Lodieta believes the simple facts
You do the best of what's given you
When she wakes up she starts again
No sign of a complaint
Paints on that smile for all to see
Even when what is shown is ain't
Lodieta is a hidden treasure
A Diamond in the rock
Though when the sun does catch her sparkles
Then Life pauses to take stock
Lodieta has mixed history
Loving Family, twisted Fate
Through it all she still stands tall
Never learnt the word named Hate

When I am full of exasperation
When temper seems to climb
I think of Lodieta
My anguish seems a crime
Yes we all have our histories
Some better than the rest
It's about how you deal with it
Lodieta handles best
When all seems dark
I reach for Gie
When I feel lonely
She sits with me
Oh Lodieta, we've travelled different paths
Though both led to led to where meant to be
We've descended lows and enjoyed the highs
Upon the road of Destiny

Lodieta dreams of happy things
Now I dream of happiness to
She teaches patience with a laugh
Finally I get the clue
Lodieta is quite shy
Once you get past her practised shell
She has her moments, those painful times
But to others she will not tell
All my life I've sought inspiration
I found it in one known as Gie
When I reflect I am the one she's chosen
Then I know true ecstasy

Lodieta I truly love you
You are the person I aspire to be
So many know you but don't know you
They just know your shell called Gie
You are the enigma that I puzzle
The soothing balm to treat my woes
When conflicts rage all around me
I look to you and peace it shows
You will never truly know
Just how special you truly are
You have strength to change my world for better
Even though you chance from far

When Angels cried their tears did fall
Fell on ground and plant it grows
Became a symbol of all things special
Became what I call Special Rose

YES

I am in love – that lethal drug
I am addicted and all can see
My future world has changed forever
Just because what you mean to me

I wake up sweating when you're unhappy
I rush to end things so we can chat
In lonely times I stare at photos
Trying to work out where heads at

I do not ask you for your body
For that is something should freely give
This is something way much deeper
This is reason why we live

We have had our good times
We have had our bad
Though through all the changes
You're still the one to make me glad

When knowing that you're hurting
And I can't comfort with a touch
Never have I felt so hopeless
That indeed does tell me much

We'll fight it all, what Fate may bring us
We'll stand together in mass crowd
We'll grow closer with the pressure
We'll one day shout out loud

Yes – before I had that feeling
This time, however, know it's true
Changed my world and changed my thinking
I am in love – in love with you

———

WHEN THE LOVE IS STRONG
With Lodieta Sumayo, my dream sharer

Now our day is over, come my Darling sit here right next
to me. We will talk of each other's day, talk of meant to
be. The sun will lower through the window, the dark
replace the blue. Still we'll sit here talking together,
talking about the world, the world of me and you.

And when sleep calls we'll go together
Unto a different world
A place of peace, a place of hope
A place together curled

When tomorrow comes and my eyes do open I want
but just one sight. When I see you there tranquil
bathed, then my day starts right. Hiccups come and
hiccups go, to us familiar friend. Nothing serious and
we're soon back laughing, our joy will never end.

And when sleep calls we'll go together
Unto a different world
A place of peace, a place of hope
A place together curled

You gave to me a loving Child, something I've never had.
To be truthful it left me scared, but is best I've ever had.
I know I drive you crazy, I bounce from wall to wall. Yet
I am so truly grateful, you stick with me despite it all.
I wish I had a Golden Wish that I could give to
you. A wish you want so deep, a moment that could
be just your own. A space for you to keep.

And when sleep calls we'll go together
Unto a different world
A place of peace, a place of hope
A place together curled

When Love is Strong there are no worries, only choices on
what we do. None are single for we're a partnership, all are me
and you. Yes our Child does take front stage, wouldn't want it
any other way. Though tonight within our dreams, is you and
I that lay. Morning comes and we are three, in sleep we are
but two. Nothing wrong or guilt felt, it's just what lovers do.

And when sleep calls we'll go together
Unto a different world
A place of peace, a place of hope
A place together curled

STRAWBERRY SUN

Let me take you by the hand
And lead you to a far off land
With Apple fields and Strawberry sun
Where Unicorns roam and play for fun

Nothing dies here
There is no pain
It is a land of eternal hope
Where you heal and grow again

I've been there once before my friend
But alas I could not stay
For I had to return to my home
Until for my sins I pay

Now I've paid them
And you I know have none
Let me introduce you my dear
To the land of the strawberry sun

PAINT FOR ME THE PERFECT PICTURE

Paint for me the perfect picture
Show to me what is sought
Place before me an image blessed
Create for me a perfect thought

Show to me with your vision
A soul so caring when revealed
Give to me a source of comfort
Lay upon me until I yield

Paint a picture of thought and wishes
Reveal an image that is blessed
Sooth my mind in its beauty
As I lay my Head down to rest

Sing to me your deepest feelings
Whisper gently that you care
Caress me with a picture perfect
Allow to dream of when you're there

WHEN TWO HEARTS

So do rise from troubled sleep
Depart from rest before the Birds do sing
Yet alive and filled with hope
To see what joy your words do bring

Anticipation is paramount
Like a vessel I do fill up
Sustained by you in completion
Rehydrated from loving cup

I dream that dream of a thousand lovers
That of hope and expectation
To a union of two Hearts
The dream passed down from generation

The one for some that has reward
For the fortunate it does bind
To them barriers are just stepped over
When two Hearts are of the Loving kind

Time is precious but so is right
Right time to do things to make it last
Both have a future spent together
Both had pain in the past

I love you my Darling – know that true
Love you my sweet come what may
Will still love you in years to come
Will love you till my dying day

So to this world we are shown
To this world we've just begun
Longer is the journey together
Then that day when we are one

———

JERICHO WALL AND LODIETA

I sit upon the rubble
That was once my Jericho Wall
Love did blast it trumpets
My defences they did fall

I'd built them with a purpose
To keep things way outside
One did whisper and they did crumble
From you I couldn't hide

Not everything is sorrow
I now realise
Pleasure also resides out there
I find to my surprise

You went Greek and did employ
Your Trojan horse and did destroy
I celebrated, thought I'd won
You got inside and showed me fun

In 1066 you were the Normans
Smaller force but better plan
Struck me down with Cupids arrow
Now I love the one that can

At Agincourt you were the Bowmen
Struck my armour fearful blow
When I charged you were ready
Taught me something I didn't know

1815 and you were Wellesley
Against my character Bonaparte
You gave to me my Waterloo
Crushed my empire to make new start

I could go on with tales of smartness
But same result every time
You got me beaten by our thinking
In my eyes you are sublime

Gracious are you as the victor
Out thought – out fought and I am glad
My Jericho Walls came tumbling down
Shown me best times ever had

I SAW YOUR FACE, I
SAW THE FUTURE

I saw your face, your smiling face
I heard your voice I longed to hear
We laughed when met on Internet
It brought you somehow near

Now we do talk often
In typed and spoken word
The feeling's fine because you are mine
To doubt it is absurd

When we spend an hour it goes like minutes
So much we have to say
We never run short of a fun retort
You really make my day

Time will pass so very quickly
Until I sit upon your land
Then you can show the places know
My life will seem so grand

Three of us will make a fuss
A fuss about each other
A Family strong that has no wrong
A success within the cover

A Book of Hope, a book of faith
Faith that good can win
We do believe and so shall receive
That longed deep within

To see you and to hear you
Is but a stepping stone
To what is planned now in your land
Where we will then call Home

I saw your face, I saw the future
I saw what lies ahead
No three souls with similar goals
A loving team instead

SIDE BY SIDE

When times are we stand together
Each a shield for others 'Blind side'
Back to back within the maelstrom
We fight together with Love and Pride

When flood of hatred rages around us
We become an Island in that sea
Granite rock standing proudly
Believing in what's meant to be

Through fields of fire
A bond is sown
Through the hatred
A passion grown
When battle pauses we seek each other
If not by sight then sound and feel
To reassure that don't stand alone now
Know this partnership is forever real

This battle it will last us a lifetime
For as foes defeated new replace
We will face them from all directions
We will conquer with purity and grace

Side by side but turn when needed
Team tactics come to the fore
Thrust and counter, defence and counter
Love and Pride forever more

WHEN I HAVE THE WORDS

When I have the words that I cannot share
It is because that you are not there
For so private is language spoken
When is said a feelings token

When I have words that stay silent
That silence screams in volumes much
Foe silence is because I miss you
Lack of words is lack of touch

When I have words that describe me
Tell a world just how I feel
That lay it out on a table
That makes it smile and make it real

When I have words to say I love you
When three words can battle through
When I have words that convince you
When I have words that say so true

AND SPEND THE DAYS TOGETHER

Come said you and so I came
Walk with me and so we walked
Sit with me and we then sat
Talk with me and us talked

Have no regrets for accommodating
Partnerships are give and take
How one feels in compromising
Is the reason teams do break

Not of you and not of me
Though outside can't view what see
Behind the screen we erect
Leave our story circumspect

We both know the course we've planned
Just like both do know the weather
Just batten down and wait the passing
Both love and laugh and spend the day together

When waves do rise we do surf them, when trapped
deep we find the hole. Nothing man made can
beat the spirit, the burning spirit of the soul.

Then I spoke and you did listen
I reached out, you grasped my hand
Then I dreamt and you dream with me
One will settle on distant land

Then you gave another that loves me
I return and love them back
For two souls make not a Family
You add a third and build the stack

We converse and converse together
About our cultures and our weather
We understand, learn from each other
We are stories that share a cover

I offer love and you give me love
I care for you -you care for me
I give you hope, you give it freely
Together find our sanctuary

When waves do rise we do surf them, when trapped
deep we find the hole. Nothing man made can
beat the spirit, the burning spirit of the soul.

BREAKING WALLS

'Breaking walls and healing Hearts
My task is so fulfilling
If you have blockage towards your happiness
I have a tool for drilling

I am the handy man that can
Try to fix you – make you good
Understanding through true listening
Giving feedback understood

And when you feel you're out of options
Checked your Well and found it dry
I will lead you to sweet water
Advise new options and reason why
For saying without explaining
Is just hot air to me
Let sink in then begin
Chapters Two and Three

I am the Teacher who doesn't teach
Alter ego fits me better
If can't meet you face to face
Then phone call or a letter

I am your wounds though them moved on
I am your future scars on show
Of current pain I have past knowledge
Of what you speak I know

When you feel no-one understands
I will be there to hold your hands
When you feel that need to cry
I'll hold the cloth to dry your eye
Everyone needs someone
To sometimes share a weight
With empathy I will help carry yours
For is my future and is my fate

Breaking walls and opening dreams
I'm living mine and want to share
Have found something that can't be bought
That is true love mixed with care'

If every adult said this to every child
Through them all things could change
Passing it along as times went on
Our present would seem strange

EYES

I stared down at the cold blank screen
Where moments before you had been
Made me realise how much I miss
The warmth of your tender kiss

Though we're talking far apart
We are closer than the start
Counting down to when again
We can stand in summer rain

When I look into those deep dark eyes
My Heart it soars, my soul it flies
Up on high in clear blue sky
To be with you and at your side

Behind those jewels with no surprise
I feel a love so worldly wise
If you want to see the thrill inside
Then look at me, look in my eyes

I then sit back and I close mine
Dream the dreams that are divine
Can smell you, touch you in my head
We're not alone but joined instead

These words I say are what I feel
Waiting for time when see for real
In the flesh and not just call
Into those eyes will again I fall

Our Daughter too is just like you
That twinkle I do see
She has too a pure heart true
Both in the one that belongs to me

Glistening orbs, sparkling orbs
The gateway to your soul
There tenderness and promised bliss
Of a Family true and whole

L.Y.F.

I say to you, you say to me
We say three words together
We say in dark, we say in light
Love You Forever

You came to me in my blackness
I reached into your light
Speaking in your daytime
As I sit in my night

Time has passed since were together
In the physical
Will come again both do know
True Love conquers all

You and I plus ours make three
A Family true and tight
To our home once more return
In land with Sun so bright

Those three words now seem absurd
For they don't fully say
What I feel and know what's real
I'll love you forever and a Day

CALL OF THE WILD

The call of the Wild is beckoning me
But stuck inside where don't feel free
The freshness of the air I miss
Manufactured has no bliss

To stretch my legs and see the sight
Of outdoor life does seem my blight
Electric smell and electric hum
What I wonder have I become?

The needles of breath inside chest
When the cold air chooses rest
Before exploding into vapour
A hard lesson would now savour

I yearn a life of hot and humid
While above me hovers Cupid
I know that this sounds somewhat stupid
For my true Love there waits for me

The trickle down neck of water stream
At this moment seems a dream
Instead silent stamp to keep feet feeling
The night covers reluctant peeling

Here sounds so harsh – it sounds so bad
But from this place no choice I had
Don't want four walls to enclose
No strange commuter perfume disturbing nose

Call of the Wild is so strong
Feeling 'inside' doesn't belong
Seldom Tan here, Hot or Cold
Pasty skin is my story told

I miss outside in every season
Changes of factors are my reason
With thought and planning plus some care
In new place I can be there

Different climate – different views
Different languages - different news
But outside with Mom and Child
Can then answer call of the Wild

LINK OF GOLD

The coals do glow and the heat does rise
The pounding thumps within my head
From ingots of steel links are formed
There grows a chain from my life fed

The chain of life is of many links
Each is joined to make them strong
Moulded from that flame of feeling
Each does know where it belongs

A master smith is at work
He is skilled in his trade
He crafts with skill and crafts with thought
He made a link that would not fade

Somewhere within this chain of life
There now sits a link of Gold
It stands apart and stands out proudly
For it is the link of our story told

The brightest link and most precious link
The link that joined two spirits true
Bonded until then two different lives
It joined the paths of me and you

Of Gold for it will not tarnish
Of Gold for it will not fade
Of Gold for it is to me so special
Of Gold for shone when choice was made

TOUCH THE HEAVENS

I sought the Ying to my Yang
Searched for the white to my black
Then met you and pulse did race
Felt I would have a heart attack

We run through the swaying corn fields
We do swim in mountain pond
We then smile and we do laugh
We tell of memories of which we're fond

I hold your hand and you hold mine
We dance and skip, we float in air
Hug and kiss then hug again
Live in a world with no-one there

We pause and glance up to the sky
Then we bid the earth goodbye
We soar and soar into the ether
We touch the Heavens and hear Angels cry

They do look and tears do flow
Tears of joy run down their face
To see such love in mortal beings
Is why their lord made Human Race

MET IN MELLOW MOVING CLOUD
(Magpakailanman at isang araw)

You were a stranger now more than friend
You were a start but have no end
We met in moving mellow cloud
Now that chance to speak out loud
You accepted me but with release
If I became that didn't please
Never had the awkward squeeze
Just that chill of spine and weakens knees

We met in cloud that was confusion
Made it real with our infusion
Took a past and made solution
Now lead paired life with absolution
And in the memories shared together
Things have grown and now a picture
I never knew the joy of a love letter
Until met my equal, maybe better

So when you lay your head to sleep
Think of me and that thought keep
We've come too far and now in deep
To eye another with more than peep
We laugh, we cry, we hurt together
We now discuss our different weather
We joke when spoke about a bloke
That with his talk can sleep invoke

We were both lost but then we found
Were better off when shared our ground
Maybe to some we did astound
But slowly we turned that around
For what is love but pure feeling?
When chest does ache and heartbeat reeling
Smitten once but now forever
With you and Daughter whom both clever

Fourteen of two is not so new
But this can sometimes change
When with sense of wit I do now pit
To you a verse so strange
Happy Valentine's my love
I miss you oh so much
But I feel strong for not that long
Until again I feel your touch

CAN'T FEEL DOWN

I can't feel down with you around
No matter how I try
You pop up and sad pops out
Too quick to say Goodbye

You make me laugh, you make me smile
I love the games we play
You focus me with your energy
Though in your shy own way

You make me smile until it hurts
Laugh until it croaks
Amaze me with your understanding
Leave my crying with your jokes

My day might test my patience
Stupid things take new proportions
Then one word or sticker sent
Has my mood in new contortions

Yup can't feel down with you around
Despite how hard I try
Love and laughter fills my world
You are the reason why

When you are happy then I'm ecstatic
When you are down I have a mission
When I am clueless, give direction
When I need, give - no condition

Thank you, you for being you
Though you probably don't know why
Thanks for being there for me
To teach me how to fly

SWEETEST

Sweetest is the desire to hold you
To touch and feel that thing called 'LOVE'
Sweetest are the message sent
For they are blessed from those above

Sweetest are our dreams to come
Sweetest our the memories of our past
So is our bond and understanding
Sweetest is our hope to last

Sweetest is that simple feeling
Sweetest is that gentle touch
Sweetest the knowledge that you care
Sweetest a drink from loving cup

Sweetest is that treasured moment
Of when we bond and when we share
Sweetest is when we forget
This whole world and what is there

CHAINS AND WALLS

The sweetest is a contented soul
The warmest is a fulfilled heart
The fullest is a life of love
The purest is a romance at start

All my questions have been answered
All the doubts now put aside
All my feelings now unleashed
All is open with no need to hide

That weight of burden in my world
Was truly tested when I met you
Had chains and walls around my heart
Were smashed to pieces with feelings true

You have freed an imprisoned man
You have shown a path so clear
Just one more hurdle to overcome
Because of you I want you near

IN TIME OF JOY

I miss you most in times of sharing
A time of union and of caring
Cold is a bed when filled with one
Thoughts and talking seem undone

I see you through Technology
Disconnect and then just me
No smiling face to upturn my lips
Just rewind and replay those clips

In time of joy all is fine
You are with me, you are mine
In time of joy we forget the present
In time of joy do ride the crescent

Now is the time I miss you most
A birth of Son and Holy Ghost
I could be one and you the other
For at this moment we share no cover

Absence makes the Heart grow fonder
Did that writer truly miss?
For no distance however covered
Replace the pleasure of just one kiss

We say 'Goodnight and see tomorrow'
That thin veneer to hide our sorrow
'Darling' a word I've seldom said
Leads to others within my Head

For to me is not lightly spoken
Is a 7 letter pure Love token
A Token given for later claim
No simple statement within a Game

Darling I love you
Mockers take what you will
Bend and bow but never broken
Darling before and Darling still

Ha those Mockers scent victory
Yet they figure not our Destiny
Time of union and circle close
Despair for some when truth it shows
Darling we are meant to be
Both know the word called Destiny

At time of cold let me blanket you
In time of stress make you smile
When you need guidance let me speak
When are tired I'll provide that mile

In all this writing of ramble line
I try to say you are divine
Not to others but are to me
We set our goal and will always be

You are the World I sought so long
The perfect words to my favorite song
Just one reason I rise each day
Another chance to hear what you do say

Immortal is an oft said quote
Invulnerable to that others tote
That is us my future Wife
To coin that phrase 'such is Life'

So reduced I say in our phase 'Despair'
For I am with you and you are there
Separate beds but not forever
Is the time cometh soon
Now and for always we'll lie together

That warmth will banish whatever cold
That joy will speak as yet untold
Of far flung bodies placed apart
Who were still joined by just one Heart

Goodnight my Darling, sleep content
You asked for comfort and I was sent
Likewise I asked and came to me
The one who was my Fantasy

Ngayon at palaging nasa iyo at atin

Rejoice, Rejoice that airless feeling
You leave me breathless and Heart still reeling
Giddy am I in rapture found
Have found my soul mate on solid ground

Hark those Trumpets in glory blast
Sound out loud and meant to last
For I am complete for all to see
Pitch it high for Eulogy

One soul, one being has found feeling
That golden second that leaves one reeling
No history of before
Just a future to explore

No more nights just sent alone
Now cast aside that Granite stone
For is now velvet and Ermine lined
Cold and sterile left behind

Hear those chords of me at rest
Not of slumber but of zest
Nothing now matters but to get you Home
They show their worth but 'when in Rome'

To sleep now is just fantasy
My body full of what you mean to me
Tingle does the nerves free will
I love you once and once is still

In time of joy there is no choice
When found that tone within your voice
That special tone oh divine
Sleep well my Darling two dreams do shine

BESIDE YOU

When you work I work beside you
I try to help and ease your load
When you travel I walk beside you
You shall never travel a lonely road

When you hunger I will feed you
When are thirsty give you drink
When you are resting rest beside you
Share the thoughts we both do think

When you sleep I sleep beside you
Wrapped together in loving arms
When you wake I wake before you
Just to check that day has charms

And in each moment that I am with you
I laugh and gently hold you near
Lift you up when you seem tired
Speak of love within your ear

For I am with you now, forever
We made a bond and swore a pact
I've joined with you until the Sun burns out
From now to then I will make this act

Never once feel you are alone
Never feel that I have just gone
Always know that we are together
Always believe in this love so strong

For when I work you are beside me
When I falter you pick me up
When I hunger your love feeds me
When am dry give friendship cup

When I sleep you are there with me
When I awake you're still there too
When I doubt you do convince me
When I am stale give something new

IN WARM MOONLIGHT
A shuffle with 'Gie' Sumayo

When all is dusted in introductions
Then is time for Truth to start
8 letters, 3 words take on new meaning
For are love letters from the Heart
We met, we chanced, we went further
We bonded, we gelled, and we became a pair
Increased communication and attention
We miss the time when you're not there

I come from the wrong place so they say
But this is not where I grew up
I've moved around before settled here
Spent too long a day in the stirrup
A town is but a place name
Not all who live there change their views
I am still within that barefoot boy
Too poor for coat and pair of shoes

Lady I met you out of the blue
Yet something said that we were similar
Time moved on and together we moved on
Now you are that presence so familiar
I have two left feet
You are so right
So we can't dance in normal way
So let's shuffle together in warm moonlight

We come with nothing and leave with nothing
So why do some seem to judge so quick
Just because they have no self contentment
They walk around with a 'golden' stick
You and I are simple folk
No Fame and Fortune turns our head
Judge not others by our 'statuses
We walk together where Fate has led

You and I will beat the mockers
You and I won't play their game
You and I will laugh at their efforts
You and I we are the same
The oddball couple from different places
The Dreamers that "really have no clue"
Dreamers dream and Dreamers chase
This wrong town boy has set sights on you

Lady I met you out of the blue
Yet something said that we were similar
Time moved on and together we moved on
Now you are that presence so familiar
I have two left feet
You are so right
So we can't dance in normal way
So let's shuffle together in warm moonlight

THAT HOLDS YOUR HEAD

When you see above a star
Smile at it for it is me
When upon you feel a breeze
It is I kissing tenderly

When you sense a sunny day
Wrap yourself within its glow
Though distance means that we're parted
I am here and you should know

When you laugh you make me smile
For true joy is not just sound
It does travel on forever
Truest love it has no bounds

When at rest, rest in comfort
Lay with peace upon your bed
Embrace the pillow that is beneath you
For it is I that holds your head

CLOSER

I take some steps just to explore
The places that not been before
Each does take me closer still
To the place that's in my will
The call it echoes strong and loud
That I am its focus leaves me proud
The 'Chosen one's this time around
Places me upon hallowed ground

Heard of Love and read the Books
Dismissed it all as fantasy
Then came you to shine a clue
At what is real and just can be
Now float on air without a care
Engulfed in the divine
My Blessings know as we do grow
Closer from when you were just my Valentine

GOLDEN

When our time is right our future Golden
Just like your Sun and loving way
Sleep together in security
Tomorrow will be a fantastic day
When I can touch you, feel your caring
All the love you give to me
Then begins our real shared journey
Then begins our fantasy
Golden is the skin tone you're wearing
Golden is the inside you
Golden thoughts you created
Golden wishes I will do

Life was Black but then came sunshine
Did at first make it Brown
Continued shining upon this creature
Turned it Golden and gave it Crown
Golden is our child we nurture
Though a child is no longer
You and she worked before me
Now an Adult - smarter, stronger
Golden are times we spend together
Golden laugh and Golden smile
Knowledge that my fate is Golden
Keeps me happy from far off mile

Golden dreams and Golden hopes
Have left me unto you beholden
I forget what was my history
When think of you and future Golden
Golden is the air around you
Golden is my love for you
Golden is the ring I offer
Golden the promise made to you
In Golden days and Golden years
We will laugh with Golden tears
You came to me, a Fantasy
Now my life is Golden

L

    I

       F

         E

THE POET WITH THE STICK

Yes my Orbs are no longer normal
Yes these days I can't read so quick
Yes my body is somewhat complex
Yes I am the Poet with the Stick

If you love something that makes you happy
There is no reason for that to change
Even if in Life things happen
That leaves you in a World that's strange

Yes I am now Epileptic
Triggered by electric screens
Yes I am adapting to use them
Where there's Will there's always Means

If you have people that support you
Just by knowing how much they care
Then the conviction of the Body
To survive bad things can be there

Yes my Ticker doesn't run full function
Parts of it decided to stop
Yes I am now a Pill popper
13 a day but looking to drop

If one is determined then anything's possible
It's just a case of never quitting
I am the half Blind epileptic Poet
But things are fine from where I'm sitting

Yes I've had both a Heart attack and Stroke
Yes I admit that they changed me
Took me from what I've known
Placed me where I never dreamed to be

I am not one for sympathy
I am not one for pity
I am one who is chasing Dreams
I am the one that can write a ditty

IN SOME M.I.A PLACE
(In some Missing now in action)

Hours sleep then snap awake
Words racing round the head
Toss and turn but just calories burn
Reach for pen instead
A way to go as lines do flow
The ink does dance and race
Have been before will again I'm sure
In some Mn.i.a. Place

When body finally takes control
Telling Mind to shut and quit
The wave of relief would be ecstatic
If one was aware of it
Missing in action on sleeps campaign
Going AWOL during tour
Not a thing that one does want more than once a night
Nor in future want much more

The world it seems so different
When the Sun has gone away
The atmosphere confusing
When night creatures come out to play
The smells become much sharper
To compensate for sight
Wish was choice to enjoy the experience
Of insomnia at night

To be able to view this landscape fully conscious
Appreciate it entirety
Mother Nature claiming back her Throne
From likes of you and me
But would then miss the charms of another sense
That provided by the eyes
Tell me why we have to sleep
Tell me one who's wise

Stinging orbs do irritate me
As hand flutters over sheet
Of paper beside my resting place
Placed precise and neat
Day and Night to enjoy both Worlds
Using sound and vision
Ecstasy I can envisage
Not In some Mn. I. A. Place on sleep mission

SOMEDAY MAYBE

Someday maybe you'll talk to me
Someday maybe will ignore desire
Someday maybe you'll recognise me
Someday maybe pride wont fire

Someday maybe you will doubt
Someday maybe you will enjoy
Someday maybe you'll realise
Someday maybe won't play with toys

Someday maybe you will suffer
Someday maybe when feel alone
Someday maybe you will regret
Someday maybe when come off that Throne

Someday maybe you will account
Someday maybe will compromise
Someday maybe you will grow up
Someday maybe you will grow wise

I SWAM WITH DOLPHINS
– AND DO AGAIN

(To my Teenage infatuations and my
Soul Mate that I found after)

What is love but warmth and contentment?
Mixed with excitement and passions fires
Of dreams we can plan together
Of shared ambitions and desires
To be with someone who makes you smile
Have a soul that's twinned with yours
A mirror image of what you're feeling
Who looks beyond your flaws

So sleep not you with troubled dreams, sleep you not with fear
For I am your sword, I am your shield,
I'll protect you always dear
And worry not in waking hours, never dread of hurt and harm
For with me beside you I'll give you peace and calm
For by being with you life's moved on
It's raised to higher grounds
It has me swimming with the Dolphins
My joy and happiness know no bounds

To share my life with such as you
Is all a man could ever need
To live and laugh with you my darling
Is to my euphoria feed
For you I'd give my body
Earthly goods, my heart and soul
With your presence here beside me
Am complete at last, am whole

———

But then that day – that worst of days
You met another and moved on
And what was once a Bridal March
Became our sad Swan song
You've left my life, no second chance
Read my life story and ripped asunder
Leaving a numb and bewildered man
To now try to grasp and wonder

What was right between us
Filled me with new ambition and new hope
What you taught me about myself
Gave me the strength to cope
Guess I just ran short of your expectations
My jigsaw lacked a piece
With someone else you've found that ingredient
So to me you showed release

What more hope could I offer you?
What left did I have to give?
This knight in shining armour
Lies stricken on ground before you, lost the will to live
We had it all – or so I thought
We made things they couldn't break
So in abject sorrow and consternation
I need to get over for new beginnings sake

Alas those beautiful creatures now have to swim
Alone once more, for know within their hearts
That this soul needs time to heal its wounds
Before a new life that it starts……………..

Time moves on and changes happen
Been long a single as did I wait
Then came my true love and all was worth it
Patience needed when you follow your Fate
A bright star appeared upon my horizon
Though time does dull the sight of man
Burned through the fog of my acceptance
Smashed a lock as only you can

Breathed new life and pumped new blood
Over time you made me whole
A child was born deep inside me
With your care began new soul
To trust to love is never easy
With each layer built a stronger wall
I have found just needs right person
Then stone and mortar crack and fall

There is nothing forced and nothing false
You swept me away by being you
No lies, no promises without intent
Nothing said that is not true
How I wish this meeting sooner
So for longer we could enjoy
Though now are together will be forever
Even after body we employ

The other day I was treading water
A pod of Dolphins did appear
With clicks and chirps and tail walking
Gleefully they swam to near
We touched, we nudged and swam together
Deep in knowledge that each would stay
I swam with Dolphins and do again
You made this happen and we do play

Somehow I think that we're connected
You, I and Dolphins are meant to be
We share a love, we share happiness
In strange way share Destiny
We will ride their chariot in the Heavens
Whilst on earth lives our legacy
When time comes they will join us
And this chariot is built for three

Celestial souls riding the Heavens
For eternity and a day
When I met you they came back to me
Now you and I with Dolphins play

SOUL SPIRITS
(Internet great friends)

Soul Spirits, they wander freely
Not encumbered on the physical plane
Soul Spirits know when find a partner
Find a way to pleasure gain

The bodies may live so far away
Be the side of Earth
Does not matter nor is important
They persist for know the worth

May never meet face to face
Yet inside you are together
Communication is all that matters
Soul Spirits bond and bond forever

When you meet your spirit partner
Changes happen within the Mind
Feel you known them all your life
See with clarity when you were blind

Soul Spirits search for their partners
Soul Spirits never do fatigue
Soul Spirits are a hidden treasure
You and I will cause intrigue

PLASTIC EYES

Me I've got somewhat different eyes
Both have a plastic lens
Originals got somewhat cloudy
Nearly drove me round the bend

Two quick ops within six months
Put a firm end to that curse
A pad over eye for a short while after
Now back to writing verse

Not exactly common
For people of my age
But I am greedy, got problem early
Now can get back to earning a wage

But the best advantage of them all
Is my wallet no longer leaner
For instead of forking out for dearer eyewash
I can use a cheap glass cleaner!

'MAN FLU'

I am poorly and I am sad
Have blocked up nose and heavy chest
I have 'Man Flu' that dreaded curse
I need your attention so forget the rest

I have 'Man Flu' and I am suffering
Women out there call it a Cold
Yet I am suffering and a grumbling
I am a victim yet not untold

My Nose it runs and Eyes do water
Incapable of any work
'Man Flu' is so devastating
Your inattention drives one berserk

A man with 'Man Flu' is a sorry picture
A man that's lost that inner fire
A cough, a sneeze does need attention
Please don't mock and please desire

GOLDEN STAR

The Red of morning sunrise
Borders the Blue of open sea
The Golden Star upon Whiteness
The place I wish to be

The soft, soft sands so inviting
Palm trees in their splendour
The welcome of the one I seek
The feelings warm and tender

Children shrieking, running round
Finding things to please
Me a product of concrete jungle
See this as release

Yes I would gladly trade
The comforts I'm told I need
To live in place where community important
Where no judgement of one's creed

Some might call it basic
Base is from which we grow
Aspirations are still abundant
From healthy seeds you sow

Too long I've spent in this First World
Drip fed the tales of glory
Swept aside the atrocities
They are hidden story

Red and Blue, White with Gold
The draw it does increase
Only when I am there
Will I feel release

I've found my place upon this Earth
A planet hurt and torn
Found the spot that is me
Not the place where born

My future lies upon its ground
A feeling I can't hide
For amongst the people living there
My Family do reside

HEART ATTACK

The body tenses and then it jumps
Lungs take a gasp of tube fed air
A surge of energy courses through it
Whilst eyes refuse to lift blank stare

The brain still fights to keep things going
Commands its carriage to carry on
Another jolt, another breath
Now the test if will is strong

Caring people, learned people
Smoothly proceed with what they were trained
Technology and Human actions
Combine to ensure another victory gained

A blip of light runs across the screen
A whirr emits and they stand back
All are focused all determined
To beat the challenge of a Heart Attack

7 SEAS

Value every moment – each second, all you have in Life
Appreciate all you feel, all the Joy and all the strife
For all too soon it's taken from you
You get no chance to close that door
Live each experience and treasure it
For all too soon you can't explore
"Life is sweet" so often spoken
But do we appreciate just what was said?
For Life is more than just breathing
It's what goes on inside your Head
Through my time I have journeyed
Seen the sights over the 7 Seas
Have marvelled and despaired at what I witnessed
Things that hurt and things that pleased
Then I took a walk down that tunnel
And gently peeked through the Door
But I was not ready for that before me
I still want to learn and to explore
I found my "Dark Place"
Where you no longer feel the pain
Have hit the bottom level
No choice but grow again
No more News will shock me
No sadness anymore
"What doesn't kill you makes you stronger"
So recuperate and then explore
Now I greet each early morning
Relish what each Day will bring
Strangers voices are a Choir
And I, with them, to Life do sing
Yes I have travelled over 7 Seas
But since have travelled greater things
Have discovered that inner peace
Conquered doubts and my heart it sings

BORN ONE PLACE

Born one place to live in other
Met someone, now Dad, Daughter and Mother
Forget the tones of outer cover
Savour the attention of the lover
What is Home but where the heart is
What is life but full of slight twists
Adapting is the common cure gist
Learn it well and find your true bliss

When starry gaze - it is returned
Passion flows and passion burns
There's nothing like feelings that are not spurned
To give value of a love that is not to hate turned
And stay with me my sweet, sweet love
I need you more than you can know
Stick together as we get closer
With every trouble we do grow

I have mine and you have yours
We have a third who both free chooses adores
Never knew true meaning 'implores
'Til I met you on far and strange shores
World was changed and for the better
When saw your name - each single letter
You weren't offering but I did get ya
Born one place and now changed because I want there

No real stress involved - just evaluation
Guess something learned each Generation
We hold no fear of different nation
If it is a right, the situation
When love is pure and love is true
Amazing are the things can do
Never really had a clue
Until that day that I met you

AFTERGLOW

On bed of flesh I rest my head
Warm and beating, soft the cover
Gentle fingers stroke and soothe me
Tender touching from my lover
Hushed the whisper as she speaks
So full of love and full of caring
Takes me places never been
Gives release and full of daring

Two bodies rise and fall together
As in harmony do we breathe
Slow releasing from the Tempest
Moist and rumpled sheet beneath
Burned with fire did the passions
Each explored so we could know
The blissful trembling of spent body
Basking in the afterglow

Slowly drifting into shared sleep
Entwined souls now set free
Shells do mould and form together
Minds at rest for intimacy
The joining fast then slow and thoughtful
Purge the lust then pleasure give
Gift and gifted equal measures
Know full glory how partners live

Spent and sated are desires
Until return within each other
Then page written within a chapter
Within the book our future covers
Until that time I am contented
Having shared our ecstasy
For only two can make this happen
When both are true there's chemistry

Senses, memories carry me away
For I have felt and now do know
The ultimate in bodily pleasure
When one enters Afterglow

FOOTFALLS OF FORGOTTEN FOES

Was once a lad but now a man
My anger has subsidised
Maturity has made new me
Thus a life provided

Once battles fought that came to nought
Rage my only fuel
Stood in danger to fight a stranger
My pain a therapy tool

Then one day I realised
I woke to sanity
I'd become one quite undone
My arch nemesis was me

Crawled inside to remove that pride
The one that held me down
Learnt to share both love and care
Made a smile from a useless frown

I find now can laugh at myself
At the fool I was before
Caught within a dark, dark room
Just could not see the door

The faces have all gone now
I never knew their names
Just a foolish male with foolish view
Playing foolish games

So many days, so many nights
So many years ago
Lost are they in the mists of time
Footfalls of forgotten foes

———

LET SOFT MUSIC PLAY

The day is over, the work is done
If only for today
So sit at home, relax a while
And let soft music play

Tomorrow is another project
So wait till then to think
Enjoy tonight in relaxation
In peaceful bliss do sink

Life is sweet when workload is over
Provided not taken home
For that place is your Sanctuary
It's where spirit's free to roam

Cherish rest, enjoy the thought
Of a place to find calm
A time to ponder on important things
And the world is in your palm

Yesterday was like today
Future events unplanned come what may
But here and now you control
So let soft music play

NATURES RUBBER

Plastic lenses and half sight
Each eye has left half but not the right
Drew a line down both centres
Then Natures Rubber became inventor
Not from birth for had good vision
It was a Stroke that led this mission
Though still my orbs look good to serve
For it attacked my Optic nerve
So apart from Glasses no-one would know
The frustration of a left field show
Other things have also gone
Night and distance judgement now don't belong
Ever read a sentence that jumps up and down?
Between three lines – it makes you frown
Still not so bad in the bigger scheme
For can still type and can still dream
Not so tragic when I still can see
Those that are worse off than me
So all I ask when you read this prose
Is to allow for what does not show

FIDDLE ME DUMB

Fiddle me dumb and Fiddle me free
Fiddle a dance around Horse Chestnut Tree
It's losing its leaves in strong autumn breeze
Showing the Conkers that soon fall to me

I will then open and take out the seed
Then some string and a skewer are all that I need
Threaded and knotted now ready to swing
How many victories each one will bring

No cheating by Baking, nor Vinegar soaks
All these are fallacies and all are a joke
The skill is the choosing added to swing
Luck is a factor in which one will win

Now stare at spiked orbs, waiting to fall
How many can gather? Just one or them all
Whatever the Harvest this game will I play
You're never too old for them Conkers, whatever they say

Trust your opponent to not hit your hand
As bravely you offer your Conker and still stand
Fiddle me dumb and Fiddle me free
Will my next Conker be 'a Tenner' or maybe a Three?

Whatever result – a win or a loss
It's pure entertainment with marginal cost
Takes me back to the playground
The youth that I lost

AM I

Am I the dream that I seem
Do I seem your perfect Dream?
Does this feeling rise above
If all are yes then this is Love

Does pulse race when heard my voice
Do you stop and make your choice
Does morning seem so far away
Until can meet for another day

Do your days seem longer when we aren't talking
Does your step have spring when you are walking
Do worries half when you do share
Does comfort come because I care

I ask these things because what feel
I trust my feelings and they are real
I thank the ones that are above
Because for me I have found Love

Am I convinced that you love me?
Yes I am for what you do
Stay beside me when things did happen
Stayed beside with Love true

Am I blessed – the answer's obvious
Blessed beyond what I deserve
Nature played a trick on me
You stayed beside and did not swerve

Am I writing yet can hardly see?
Yes I am for I feel strong
Knowing that we are together
Knowing I am where I belong

AT FIRST

At first I was a granite wall
Love and trust, I shunned it all
Promised myself after too much pain
That open feelings won't rise again

Then came you

I bounced around with trust and feeling
All too often left me reeling
Betrayed, bewildered, so confused
They took me in and abused

Then came you

Every hurt it built a shell
A protection from a living Hell
If didn't want then couldn't hurt
If no stories then no dirt

Then came you

Belief in someone is something new
To commit I didn't do
To think of Future more than one
Is a choice that's just begun

For then came you

Upside down and in and out
Never knowing to laugh or shout
Finding Trust is so revealing
Of support I've been concealing

Until came you

Now a journey, now a plan
Now adventure in different land
Now a hope to boldly reach
Now a History to a child teach

Because came you

Prophecy or Destiny
All I know is that I found me
The buried me, afraid to show
Now declared and with it glow

At last came you

A EULOGY TO LIFE

Today's the day for reflection
Today's the day for observation
Today's the day for decision
Today's the day to start again
If life was just a passing moment
I guess it would not matter much
But it is a 'one time offer'
So experience it and negatives don't bother

And no one said it would be easy
No one said that fate was kind
Everything does have a purpose
Though escapes a bewildered mind
What occurs has a purpose
And what changes makes you strong
Each and all that astounds you
Are building blocks to get along

Through my life have made mistakes
But no lasting hurt was incurred
Never one for being silent
Am not the type to be not heard
Troubles come and troubles go
Just like love and friends
Wave good bye to disappointment
For the purpose it never ends

Been a single soul for so long
For a match still wait to meet
But dreams cost nothing so still dreaming
There's someone out there to make me complete
Health has dealt me a savage blow

But absorbed and get along
Compensation, I found friends
With their support can stay strong

And no one said it would be easy
No one said that fate was kind
Everything does have a purpose
Though escapes a bewildered mind
What occurs has a purpose
And what changes makes you strong
Each and all that astounds you
Are building blocks to get along

So through it all I still say resolute
Willingly will suffer strife
Hurt and rejection are fuels to feed you
And I appreciate this thing called life
It is why we are here
Envelop and it will prove you right
Treasure like your perfect partner
Acknowledge and your world is bright

And no one said it would be easy
No one said that fate was kind
Everything does have a purpose
Though escapes a bewildered mind
What occurs has a purpose
And what changes makes you strong
Each and all that astounds you
Are building blocks to get along

ACROSS THE MILES - COMMUNICATION, NARRATION

Across the miles
I see your smiles
Yours and hers and theirs as well
Despite the distance creates a spell
Lifts me cheerful
Never fearful
Until we stand together
You said, she said, they said things
Little notes, anecdotes, closer do they bring
Communication, narration, we seem to share a room
Shed a clue to a point of view
Watch the bonding bloom

Though real hours they are different
Are same inside my head
Some reading back and catching up
Create the being there instead
I hear your voice and see your face
Your animations as you talk
I could take your hand and sense your land
While together it we walk

All our worlds they are so different. Separate bubbles in Balloon.
Each has way, each has reason, each a thing to say. Where we
learnt to think as we grew up imprinted upon a mind. When
two bubbles meet, stick and greet, new treasure then we find.

One day I made a Garden, I made it just for me.
I chose a spot and cleared the rubbish.
A blank canvas for what will be.
Bought a bag, mixed seeds inside
Into the winds I scattered
Did nothing planned, just out of hand
Just doing was what mattered.

This Garden grows and beauty shows
It's something akin to Home
A place of return when I yearn
To venture and to roam
Across the Miles
I see your smiles
Yours and hers and theirs
Seen the strange that sometimes change
Though to them nothing compares

LEFT OF SEAT

Today I moved to new position
Today I sat on left of chair
Don't know why; have always been 'righty'
Just a side and so I sat there

Will today write words but left handed
I am not sure but at least will try
Always done it with right appendix
Funny really I don't know why

Shall start dressing by putting socks on
Are normally last before my shoe
Habits are so inexplicable
Habits are just what you do

Today I'll try to be understanding
Surely that can't be too hard
Bite my tongue before replying
Though inside will mark their card

Today attempt to be different
I like a challenge so that's what I'll do
Not sure though the World is ready
For today I'm something new

Today I'll try to make someone happy
Maybe even tell a joke
Not sure how they will receive it
For my humour is quite bespoke

Today will cook without a liquid
Some will say that is to broil
Same result just different wording
Like some call ground and others soil

Today, maybe, I'll double turn
Change my ways then change them back
None are ready for my metamorphosis
Don't want predictable upon my stack

BACK TO WHAT ONE WAS

As you grow you start to learn
As you learn you start to grow
Mighty might a tall person seem
Mightier is the one who knows
To look at things that do surround you
To gaze upon and understand
To have the answers to your questions
Makes Sword/Spear just fall from hand

Back to what one was before this
Back to time you had begun
Back to what one called 'The Innocence'
Back to time when one was young
I remember when things seemed daunting
I remember when things seemed strange
All around people smiled politely
All around just called it Change

Reached 'Fear Overload' when in my mid Thirties
Now early Fifties it does regress
Some say that it is me and senility
Me I say that it is progress
So many things I can have an influence
In such things can give an opinion
Alas the Earth is greater than one man
In many respects I am just a Minion

Given up reading hot headed outbursts
Have no time for extremists views
Mass Media is focused on things to shock us
Done so often now old news
Welcome back my youthful innocence
Welcome you satire addition
Laugh and mock at how we have changed us
For self-insanity is now my mission

Insanity is now new progress
Looking at what we've become
Only now it is adult serious
Not the children having fun
Back to what one was I'm wishing
Knowing that it will never be
Welcome you satire yet serious
Wrapped yourself in cloak Destiny

My Flat Earth has found new edges
The Missing Link has just been solved
All it needed was our evolution
It fell in place as we evolved
But I am not sad for this is progress
We shape the things is how we choose
What if we have one small error
Nothing changes so we can't lose

CHERRIES OR PRUNES

Never been what you'd call lucky
Should have been a human dog waste collector
For if there is the slightest on the pavement
My feet are sponges mixed with a detector

If the choice is left or right?
Red or Blue, go or stop?
Guaranteed I'll get it wrong
Do my opposite to get to the top

Butter side up or butter side down
Really is not the question you see
It's what it lands on and what it starts
Chain reaction equals woe for me

A blown fuse will start a fire
Blown bulb explodes and showers glass
On bedding, seating even carpet
Wherever I would park my – pass

Broken lace? I'd split the shoe
Busted zip? My trousers fall down
Have a slip or miss your step
Mine look like a Fairground clown

Once had a meal with a lovely girl
Cost a lot for what could have been
Did not have problem with my food
Just that of the waitress when her seen

Bought a car, looked really good
Top of range but had no clue
The make and model for which I paid
Was not just one but made of two

Mother Nature felt mischievous
When she shook my chances runes
If "life is a bowl of cherries"
Why I ask did I get Prunes?

RANDOM OBJECTS AND NODDING DOGS
(Epileptic Hallucinations)

Random Objects and Nodding Dogs
They swirl around within my head
No longer issues of concern
Acceptance and medication now rule instead

Mental issues come in many guises
All is not what is seen
I am lucky for introverted
They do not block me from my dream

'Mental Health?' now that's an issue
A subject that we choose to pass
Look around at your loved ones
Again I do the question ask

Degrees do vary in its suffering
Depression to a treatment ward
The Mind is complex in its function
One faulty wire that can't be cured

Cure no but not a barrier
For with invention some overcome
Tolerance and understanding
The Game is open – could you be the one?

GO CRAZY

DEAR VIEWERS - NORMAL SERVICE
HAS RESUMED.............

The workday is just starting
You know it will be bad
Your duties are increasing
The Boss is somewhat mad
Do you really have to do this?
Same question asked again
The needles stuck, the disc is skipping
The thought could drive insane
So let's go crazy for a moment
Stay there if like the view
Turn lists into amusement
Paper airplane with To Do
Your chair becomes a Go Kart
Your broom's a Partner - Dance
Your keyboard is a Xylophone
Duster Mic to sing romance

Paper ball wars with a workmate
Childish games now so much fun
Hours of banter just for deciding
Who goes next for coffee run?
Message a friend in same situation
Put up feet and have a sleep
Stuff that laundry that needs ironing
It's going nowhere so can keep
Who cares the Ruler's like an Ogre
So what that they are just plain lazy
They are gone playing 'power things'
Unattended? - Let's go crazy

———

The world seems right when having fun
Too boring being normal
Straight laced is for someone else
Depressing is being formal
Kick off the shoes of conventional
Tear off the jacket of constraint
Crazy is a paintbrush waiting
We've a new world we can paint

BEFORE ME

What I see, you do ask me
What I see, you want to know
What I see I will tell you
The story of how my life did grow

I see before me tasks of burden
I see before me things of joy
I see before me heavy loads
I see before me a fun filled toy
I see before me possibility
I see before me no reflection
I see before some acceptance
I see before me some rejection

What I see it is my future
What I see are things to come
What I see is no returning
Return to things that can't be undone

I see before me that I will be stronger
I see before me my spurs earned
I see before me one who's wiser
I see before me lessons learned
I see before me hope again
I see before me reason why
I see before me rewards aplenty
I see before me why I should try

What I see makes sense of nonsense
What I see I can afford
What I see is curves entwining
Lovers knot in pure silk cord

I see before me a political bubble
I see before me a 'lecture' free zone
I see before me friends and joining
I see before me opinions kept alone
I see before me lack of slander
I see before me right for silent views
I see before me pride of heritage
I see before me not posted 'news'

What I see is respect and tolerance
What I see is choice to choose
What I see no schoolyard tactics
When free vote but you did lose

PIPE AND HARP

The world I live it could be better
For am not rich nor is trend setter
It's what I make so me to blame
If discontent at my own game

Once did I a wrong step take?
Once did I almost crash and burn
Spent some time looking in from outside
Then my lesson I did learn

Walked down a path I could not ignore
Came to and banged on a strange hot door
Banged it hard though I was weak
Slowly opened with loud creak

And the hooded man said "come over here
Don't stop to think – they'll call that fear
Be big and bold and walk with me
I'll stoke your flames, I guarantee"

For a second was undecided
Hard to know when you get chided
Took a second to decide
"No Thanks my 'Friend' I'll skip this ride"

When I awoke it seemed so clear
The choice of paths is so, so near
My things have changed – been corrected
For cannot plan the unexpected
Never thought about the next day
Just lived to live and live to play
Now I know and now am wise
In return for that bad surprise

When I changed Life did too
Made some friendships and some grew
Now I know there was a plan
Now plan the future with élan

When one side plays a single pipe
The other plays the Harp
One it sounds just kind of quiet
Others' notes are beautifully sharp

BY HECK

The slap in face of sub zero temperatures
The stillness of the morn
Intake of breath to make a cloud blow out
Yet it's now past dawn

The clarity of sound is clearer
At least that's what it seems
The mugginess of balmy nights
Are far off and distant dreams

Vision slightly blurred through water
Running from one's eyes
Or fog forming on Spectacles
A thing that I despise

Encumbered by the multi layers
Bad built Robot one does look
Not your normal being
Shown in album photo book

The downside of the winter months
To balance all the good
Nature is an equal thing
That is understood

The greeting to the casual stranger
A familiar story told
Red faced people do approach each other
Say in unison "By Heck it's cold"

SPARROW'S FART

Waking before the Sparrow's Fart
Has become a kind of art
For while my love is so far apart
To stay in touch means early start

Daylight saving was a mixed blessing
For now seven hours instead of eight
But though I sleep now until one
I go to bed one hour late

I can hear the foxes do their pillaging
In the Trash Cans in search of food
Write a verse without disturbance
Starting day in happy mood

I've yet to hear a Sparrow's fart though
While that creature gently slumbers
Guess it's tiny from small body
So to hear requires numbers

A flock of Sparrows farting in unison
Would be heard but quite a shock
Certainly shock the night-time creatures
Make them pause and then take stock

Do Sparrows fart? I guess they must do
For is a function of the living
Eating food producers gassed
Then to air their gas they're giving

SUNDAY DILEMMA

Caught in that trap that comes each Sunday
Do I catch up or do I play
Things to do but need some me time
Next weekend so far away
I compromise and do some laundry
Though in truth machine did instead
But I loaded and added detergent
So I worked inside my head
Are making my meals considered chores
For could go external for lunch and dinner
Maybe even pass them by
Then my waistline would be much thinner
I am wondering whilst polishing Table
Done are printer and HiFi
Not are works but action thinking
Perhaps one day should give a try
Did the bulk yesterday, tomorrow will again will I add
Little things that keep things normal
A tidy house is never sad
Oh Sunday, Sunday you confuse me
Day of rest and all that spiel
Find I'm doing why thinking of not to
Inner laugh at the surreal
I guess I'm resting, on point of order
For I have no deadline to meet
I am relaxed and lowered heart rate
Yet still have those moving feet
Are we ever truly happy?
Being static with nothing to do
If you have found the answer how to
Please drop a line and give me a clue

———

ALAS REGRETS BUT FOREVER GRATEFUL
To my love Lodieta

Alas my thought it does wander
As wasted times do I ponder
The months and years that I forget
Unimportant for had not yet met
If things were changed in my past
We started earlier to longer last
Me an ape though to be fair
You are not and with better hair
No turning back is what I say
No living that if, what or may
For you're not here and days I count
Past is gone and plans do mount
Into a sunset warm and golden
Side by side with my beholden

On wandering sands there came a whisper
Gentle yet its warmth I felt
It summons me like a conqueror
And before it I duly knelt
That stirring air was named Commitment
It shrouded me and made its own
Gave to me a new found strength of purpose
You give me a reason to get back Home

Alas my wanting it grows stronger
Wanting to protect and hold you near
To comfort you in times of anguish
To take your hand and lead you clear
To be the Husband, the father figure
To give you both a complete once more

Consign to history time different meetings
Of when your midnight is just my four
I have to sit with warm inner feeling
While things I want do fall in place
Memories are comfort blanket
As I remember that smile upon your face
Another year has almost past
They say time flies when having fun
Bitter sweet when aren't together
Bitter sweet when I'm just one
Though we are not yet back together
In small ways wouldn't change a thing
I may not yet not hold you physically
Yet I still relish the love you bring

So thank you love - my one and only
May you have what you deserve
Though far from you, you've changed a life
Made me strong with upwards curve
Alas Regrets but forever grateful
For all have placed where am today
I am in love and am being loved
Says it all, no more to say

So Happy Valentine's Day my love
I just want to say
Alas regrets but forever grateful
Our love will last forever and a Day

GREEN SLEEVES AND RUNNING NOSE

With apologies to King Henry VIII composer,
reputedly, of that piece of music

Two Paracetamol and an extra layer
Me and it and CD player
Got 'Man Flu', a common cold
Feel like Baby so all are told

Got no strength so I am moping
But I am brave so I am coping
I'll be a warrior and bear this out
Just sit and whimper, I will not shout

Women don't seem to understand
They just get it and move on grand
Us the Stronger it hits worse
Though you shrug off like Natures Curse

Mood music is now Mucas music
Somehow not as appealing
Still it soothes and relieves
The aches that I am feeling

Tomorrow maybe I'll rock'n'roll
But that is just me breeding
Reality is Chamber music
Accompanied by my sneezing

My eyes are streaming but not through crying
The cough is getting worse
Think of me in my suffering
Oh Life is so perverse

So I listen as the notes float by
With a tissue my words compose
Try not to sneeze and wet the page
Green Sleeves and running Nose

THE TEAR DROPS TURN
TO CRYSTALS

I awoke today to lightness
A change I felt in me
A smile it came upon my face
Knew now that I was free

Those heavy dark, dark times
Now know that they are gone
Hope returns into my life
I know now you were wrong

You played me for your pleasure
You had me for your leisure
Like a Puppet you pulled my strings
Played with me like all your things

Well Puppeteer I here serve notice
Someone has cut your strings
I walk alone but with company
Free now to try new things

So my crying days are through
I'm so over you
Gone are your days of fun
When I thought you were the one
My Tears have turned to Crystals

Crystals that do sparkle
Crystals that gleam bright
Crystals of a new beginning
Crystals of a choice so right

DEAR SELF

Dear Self,
Sorry I haven't been in touch recently, how are you?
As you know it's been quite busy
How have you been keeping? I have tried to check on you
But alas, I sometimes forget
Seems so many things to do
We have recently had some unusual times
Both of us, both you and me
We really do make a perfect team
You seem to know what I do need
In return you ask for nothing
Other than fluid and a feed
I realise now that I often drive too hard
Ignore all those warnings you send to me
And then you play that card
Looking back I cannot blame you
So now we pursue a mutual dream
I think of you, you work on getting better
From both our hopes do gleam
Dear Self, please be patient
I know that I do test
Sometimes I eat what's wrong for you
Sometimes won't let you rest
I do admit that sometimes strong
When should listen sometimes get wrong
Just treat me random – like the weather
We will succeed and succeed together

Dear Self,
I hope you understand
When you read this through damaged eyes
I never meant to hurt you or cause the pain you suffered
I am more aware of what you do and how important to not forget
You are what makes me just me
Still here so no regret
You pulled me through when could have quit
More determined than I thought
Let us now enjoy our time
The time that you have bought

THOUGHT

ALBA

The Drum beat sounded across the pasture
Rolling centre then left and right
Building tempo in to inferno
Challenging to flee or fight
The Pipes they play the haunting melody
Caress the ground that notes touch
Swirl and dance like kilted players
Mystical, soulful and as such

The mist it settles upon the Heather
Creates a blanket to go again
To be burnt off with summer sunshine
Washed away with Autumn rain
The Stags belly roar in rutting season
Challenging, calling in open pasture grand
Solid stands the beast of beauty
On the windswept open land

Vivid chequers of the Tartans
Individual to the clan
Worn in honour by the woman folk
Worn with pride by the man
Spreading glow of amber liquid
Sat beside the open fire
Dulcet brogue of the Highlands
Strokes the ears – creates desire

Forget the midges so cloud forming
Forget the Celsius dropping sharp
Locked away in stone built Tavern
Entertained by voice and Harp
Alba holds a special place place in me
Though not of that country born
Rural, rugged yet spectacular
If asked to choose I would be torn

Not the lowlands for they similar places
Industrial with fretting faces
Go on North of Glasgow and Edinburgh line
To a world that is divine
Alba, Scotia, Scotland, Home
Whatever one you choose to call
I have roots from which developed
Yet when I visit for you I fall

BEGIN

Just now my Daydreams were interrupted
Reality briefly did kick in
Already missing the one I had
Waiting now for new to begin

Yesterday was kind of slow
Today, at present, seems much better
Funny how things can change
When begin the day with different letter

Begin, began or just plain start
I love the feel of something new
Gained some knowledge in what have had
What will get I have no clue

Begin to write and soon am finished
Made a short one for a change
Gone too quick this passing moment
Unexpected and somewhat strange

WHIRLY BIRD

They ride the Whirly Bird at work
Rush to desperate scenes
Giving aid and transport fast
They all know what fast time means

I am one of those proud individuals
One of those that do donate
Though never needing of their service
I somehow can relate

The scene is bad, normal can't cope
Shout goes out to have a hope
Time is crucial, land a test
In and out by air seems best

Don't you know – not supplied by Government
They spend our Taxes different way
To keep this essential modern service
By donations we do pay

Whirly Bird(s), most Counties have them
Such their value and success
Yet not valued so by Politicians
By funding them their pay rise less

The crews are working Health care experts
Maintained by experts in their field
Adapting to a new form of call out
All of them just will not yield

Whirly Bird in your livery
You symbolise a miracle to one as me
All help I'll give and gladly praise you
When see you pass know Flight Mercy

Angel Bird you Whirly Bird
Confused as you fly by
Part of me is relief you see
Part of me does cry

DRIFTING

Drifting into sleep, drifting into thought
Drifting into inspiration, when the dreams are caught
Drifting into Daydreams, Drifting into cloud
Drifting into happiness never drifting into doubt

Ever felt that pleasure?
Of when you drift away
Drifting into your own world
Never hearing what they say

Drifting into your own space
Shielded from the harm
Drifting into Utopia
Drifting into calm

Today was good for today was drifting
Today was spent in happy place
Drifting links the different worlds
Drifting fills that certain space

To drift is to live
To live you need to Drift
Drifting is so full of wonder
Drifting is a living gift

So when you next find you are drifting
Just relax and enjoy the ride
Drifting is of innocence
Drifting has no cause to hide

PURE WHITE DOVE

Upon a branch a Nightingale
It does sing the sweetest song
Others join in the background
Though its notes shine out strong

On a stem the sweetest Rose
Perfect fragrance as is such
Coloured red for its passion
Petals silken to the touch

Within an oyster sits a Pearl
Glistening in a milk like bliss
On a bed soft and gentle
A treasured object, a lover's kiss

The tottering of a springtime Lamb
As rises from the morning dew
Lovingly watched with great attention
By a proud and caring Ewe

How many ways can we describe?
That emotion we call love
For it outweighs that of hate
Tenderness is a pure white Dove

WIND OF CHANGE

Cool still water you run deep
Cool still water you soothe my mind
Cool still water so spiritual
Cool still water what pleasures will I find

Mighty Oak stands so proud
Mighty Oak a tree so stout and old
Mighty Oak tree full of history
Mighty Oak tree what stories have you told

Awesome Mountain towering onwards
Awesome Mountain piercing sky
Awesome Mountain wise old sage
Awesome Mountain tell us the reason why

Gentle Wind oh how cooling
Gentle Wind limitless with your range
Gentle Wind ever moving
Gentle Wind blowing the course of change

HAD A PENNY

If I had a penny for each time I loved you
We could forget this thing called air
Instead of me typing wistful
The three of us would be just there

Alas the good ones got there before me
Made their fortune on love prose
So mine shared with small audience
All now use and mention Rose

I get the comparison – delicate and fragrant
As one sees their one of dreams
So instead I'll build your own volume
Filled to bursting at its seams

One for you and one for other
One for Daughter and one for Mother
Just two copies will hold all
Every verse each time I fall

Fall again and each time deeper
With you both and just can't hide
Sense of purging and replacement
To those feelings had inside

If I had a penny for each time you've changed me
Would be a wonder at my Bank
Story will tell though abbreviated
When it does then you I'll thank

THE FATHER OF MY FATHER

The Father of my Father
Was a man I did not know
He was taken brutally
Before my foetus began to grow
For he was one that did serve
In that great and brutal war
Somehow lost like so many
On far and distant shore

I've never known much of him
For my Dad was young
He was born not long before
That conflict of man begun
I sometimes wonder to myself
How many are the same
Whose Fathers' Father perished
In battlefields cruel game

The Mother of my Father
Was already old when I knew her
Far too gone inside herself
To say what did occur
How many generations
Did that war cost
How many generations
Have ancestors lost?

A RHAPSODY

Each day you want it more

Some things in life do change you
Some place, some song, someone
Takes what's there and rips asunder
Replace with promise of things to come
The cause is not that clear at first
But change it does for better
Though no reason seen by those around
For no logic has a mood setter

In perverse coincidence don't you find?
It is linked to the two extremes
Involved in depth in the highs and lows
The thrills and pitfalls of chasing dreams
With dry mouth you await encounter
With heavy heart you say good bye
Not always regrets in the experience
If you know the reason why

Just like rich food or fine wine
Its consumption you'd not abuse
Sample instead in savoured measures
So its effect you would not lose
For love's a drug – you an addict
It fills and courses through your veins
A complex nirvana to a needing soul
Forever you beg, may it reign

Though when all the dust has settled
Have time to sit and see
Reflection through understanding eyes
And it still stays a rhapsody
The fix for all our bodies
The fix for all our souls
The hardest of our failures
The sweetest of our goals

BUS AND FERRY

The baggage packed but not the room
Still have some few spare seats
Leg room if you are wise
Stretch and have a sleep
Journey is a long, long one
Already you do know
Prize, however, is so important
Your future will help to grow
Bus and Ferry to new start
In the place that holds your heart
To progress your education
To one day you serve your nation

Now late teens and spread your wings
Time to find what future brings
Knowing that we're here for you
Trust and love what we must do
You have good guardians that let you grow
Shared with you all they know
Steered your course but didn't choose
For in the end is what's best for you
When one day your goals do reach
Sit and think what Mom did teach
Of all the hours worked, all miles travelled
Thanks to them that hope unravelled
Into something you could achieve
So for you, you would not grieve

If Bus and Ferry are your pathway
Then go with us beside you
We are not saying that you still need us
We are doing what parents do
Throughout your trip and much further
Will you be for what we care
Out of sight but still in mind
Whilst we breathe you will be there

POLARIS

You shine down on me and keep me true
Give direction through the haze
Always there watching over
When in search of guidance to you I gaze

Hanging there up above me
Ever present though not always seen
From my birth until I pass
You stand out bright and stand out keen

Not everyone can see you though
Have your reflection upon their face
For have to be of certain living
Only half the world receives your grace

So many names for just one vision
Depends upon to whom you speak
To me you are called Polaris
The guiding star a traveller seeks

CAPPUCCINO PROSE

Sitting, thinking, pen in hand. Listening, ticking, nodding
to the radio. Smell of coffee, all empowering. Boost to
creative thinking. Car noise outside but I ignore.

Within my bubble I am ignorant
Tap me gently the line goes
I am lost, within my own space
Caught within Cappuccino Prose

The need for writing - all consuming. The wanted
expression filling Time. Somewhere in there is
an item. Someday - Rainfalls can inspire.

Today is day I need expression
Sure you know how story goes
Energy built up inside me
Time to cure with Cappuccino Prose

When both are finished will be contented. Sitting
back - reviewed thoughts. Learning more about
inside me. Another tick mark and moving on.

All that comes is educational
With each style imagination grows
Inspiration can be varied
Welcome world of Cappuccino Prose

SILENCE IS GOLDEN

Silence is Golden yet I yearn a voice
A contact with a familiar friend
Silence is Golden yet a vacuum
Thought too deep and sorrow lend

Silence is Golden when busy in life
Is the pause to see it through?
Silence is Golden but comes with pain
Pain I get away from you

Silence is Golden when want isolation
When just want time to blank out world
Silence is Golden when is wished for
At other times a weapon hurled

Silence is Golden when want to sleep
Lack of noise to drift away
Silence is Golden in worried moments
Takes distraction and spirits play

Silence is Golden at right time
It is welcomed and it is fine
Silence is Golden when it is chosen
It can be a curse or be Divine

BAD START

When the Toast it takes a nose dive
Lands with butter down
Coffee flows across the table
A wet and golden gown
When realise your socks don't match
Your pants have got a tear
Seems like when in a rush
You actually go nowhere
When last night when things were right
Forgot to charge your phone
Now none can text you the plan
Until you get back Home

Your head it seems still full of dreams
Filled with cotton wool
Yet have to face that you'll share a space
With one you deem a fool
What do you do?
When life seems cruel
You embrace and enjoy its game
For it is weird as when appeared
It even has strange name
So smile and laugh as walk down that path
To bus stop so familiar
Take comfort in others did begin
In worse or something similar

BORN AS NORMAL

Let others have their own perception
Let them express, for their right to say
Me? I guess I was born (as normal)
I just live for brighter day

I don't do Hype, I don't do Rumour
I try (and fail) with sense of Humour
I laugh and cry, I think too deep
Some things discard and some I keep

I like to play, or sit alone
I am too lazy for Dog and Bone
I eat when hungry and drink when thirsty
Laundry Wednesday and Ironing Thursday

Shop when needed and pay my Bills
Not a great one for ringing Tills
Get my Mail, discard the junk
Every so often will do a bunk

I am no ones 'living Legend'
Nor am I a Next best thing'
Dance does me with two left feet
I can not even sing

Born (as normal) my claim to fame
Just a runner in life's game
Proud of it for of the masses
Amongst the queue for Idol passes

Not sure I want them, in all honesty
Somehow don't seem part of me
Too much work living up to expectations
Too exposed for recreations

Born (as normal) my perfect state
For is the one to which relate
Being me with no pretentions
Making lines and not inventors

On that note it's time to go
For things to do and seeds to sow
Normal things in normal times
May write something and write so rhymes

THIS ROAD WE TRAVEL

This road we travel has twist and turn
The path we venture has love and pain
The steps we take lead us into unknown
Though from each Wisdom gain
This road we travel goes on forever
Had a start but has no end
Have many strangers in its pit stops
Some ignore you and some befriend
Those that join you fall into groups
Some will part; some will stay until the end
On your road will be diversions
Some of choice and some a block
That is time to pause and think
That is time to take stock
Reconsider, reflect and change
While on our journey can rearrange

There are no rules about how you travel
Just a simple Travellers Code
Treat as you yourself wish to be treated
Never judge another just from abode
As distance passes beneath your feet
Wisdom gathers and lessons learned
Walk in quicksand and you will go under
Play with Fire - you will get burned
Whilst saying that it can be beautiful
Sights, sounds, aromas' a nice surprise
An open opinion is like a sponge
"Hey! What a bonus!! If one tries
Sometimes I meet a novice Traveller
Started their journey from different place
I like to walk with them awhile
Pass on tips and part with grace

Who knows where this road will take me?
I have Target and have a goal
Maybe that place will be on strange shore
Maybe change before am whole
That itself does not worry
I'm on my road but can change direction
Going forward is all that matters
When I am settled can come reflection
To look back and judge is somewhat easy
When done in comfort you review
Somehow then you forget the fact
What has happened created you

BROWNING

"Why are you up there my friend?"
A question had to ask
"For nearer Sun more baking done
And Browning is my task"

The logic of the idiot
Makes me want to cry
For sense does say in some strange way
Though how I don't know why

Browning is a cooking term
Sealing outside with pan hot
Browning brown will make you frown
When charcoal you have got

"I cooked the Goose that did run loose
That'll teach it to escape"
Not sure how when browning Fowl
With Head removed below the nape

Browning is a type of sauce
That really drives me crazy
For am old school so it is cool
To just call that sauce a Gravy

Browning guns are somewhat sense
If only because a name
Though using one to have some fun
A past time from which refrain

Browning is a confusing word
In what it's meant to be
Maybe I should just give up
Join the idiot up the Tree

———

CAULDRON
(like / Dislike)

And when this Cauldron of confusion
Reverts to simmer from boiling wrath
Then will people talk again
No longer led by some Experts graph
Plots, predictions, same old story
Gives a chance for someone's glory
Hype and passion a dangerous brew
Though seen before so nothing new
Though sometimes worry about those caught up
For the first time in the Spin Cup
Once the damage has been done

Is not easy to overcome
The players have gotten smarter
The masses seem somewhat dumb
Elections carried by dwindling numbers
Is this a trend that has begun?
Perhaps the folk have seen right through them
Too many vows have become just lies
Now no belief converts to absence
If don't buy then no surprise
When will those standing grasp a concept?

Nothing hard but just plain
When want to rule in Free world
Fulfil your promises and maybe do again
I am no lover of politics
Perhaps too sceptical to trust any
Still I watch and hear the newsfeeds
Where Headline acts control so many

Though who am I to make such comments?
If not wary I'll join their chart
Leaders true and sincere
Now that is rare and that is art

I know the answer!!!
It was right before me!
Let's mix this up with trending
Social voting on Social Media
Could be fun and just mind bending
Click Like / Dislike - it's all about the show
Put your thoughts to an audience you never know
They say it's for compassion
To share in someone's grief
Though is it really a new trick
To earn them some relief?
Gadgets, Gizmos, glossy functions
What's next to feature? A button War!
When did symbol replace the word?
Love, Sorry, disagree or say some more

Now take this Button and put to Voting
Imagine the fun that could be had
No more queuing at Ballot stations
Could cast your vote on phone or pad
Bored with the run up, then just Block
For will have a feature to Unlock
No more rallies or primetime slots
Get back your choices when call the shots
When you count how many are always choosing
A new Leader or some reform
Let's go crazy and track by Download
Let all things else return to norm

———

CAN I BE A RAINBOW?

Can I be a Rainbow?
That leads to someone's pot of Gold
Can I be their subject?
To their best story ever told
The greater thing than receiving pleasure
Is the pleasure one can give
In living we get many things
But to part them is to live

Today I smiled at a stranger
Bid them the joys of day
They smiled at me in return
Exchanged wishes and went their way
Simple things like recognition
A simple second in your day
Can sometimes mean so much more
When for that second their thoughts at bay

I stopped and stroked a Childs puppy
Told the boy he should be proud
His Mother beamed I spoke to son as adult
Gave her thanks to me out loud
Today took time to chat a while
With my supermarkets serving cashier
Struck up a conversation as my goods did bleep
About the weather this time of year

Am I strange because I like friendly?
Civil the name I choose to use
Though I can see times when not to use it
When approaching might seem precursor to abuse
Right circumstance, right approach
Then right is mood to share
A smile, a wink, a witty comment
A behaved cheekiness I dare

Sometimes I cannot greet in person
For the distance between us is too far
Nothing lost though in the sincerity
No matter where you are
Me? I am but a simple man
No airs and graces do I wear
Just from my soul I am happy
That happiness I want to share

TICK TOCK BEATS THE CLOCK

Love the Sunshine, brave the Rain
Live the joys and bear the pain
Praise the good things, change the bad
Embrace the happy and comfort sad

For Tick Tock beats the Clock
Beats in me and beats in you
When it stops know one knows
For different times that holds no clue

When spring runs down and pendulum stops
When no more can one do
What will be your legacy?
How will others remember you?

This is not a call for glory
Nor reminder of need to change
Just a note on living life
Within a world that seems so strange

When I was young I was taught values
Taught the benefit of peace and love
Nowadays too often hands of friendship
Seems to wear a spear tipped glove

Where has gone our age of morals
Where gone the right and wrong
Where disappeared that brief bright moment
When most of us just got along

But light shines eternal in my eyes
The hope it never dies
Too many people with loving hearts
Will create a new sunrise

I saw a Hawk circle high
Below a flock of Dove
It could not single or separate one
So ignored and flew above

I am no preacher, I am no prophet
No idol and no deity
The truth is simple, I am just one man
But I have hope that I can see

An idle dream but what are dreams
If not hope for bright tomorrow
When we can wake and enjoy our day
Not swamped with woe and sorrow

I now find myself a drifting
So back to verses start
To know when one has lost their audience
That is a humbling art

So
Love the Sunshine, brave the Rain
Live the joys and bear the pain
Praise the good things, change the bad
Embrace the happy and comfort sad

Enjoy each day and what it brings
Predicted or surprise
For Tick Tock beats the Clock
Of that you can surmise

ASPIRING MAN

An aspiring Man had dreams of glory
The imagine all would kiss his feet
One slight error in his plans
Most of them had still to meet

Aspiring Man had some good ideas
Alas ego runs amok
They liked ideas but not the person
For that man they wouldn't flock

Two years later he was despondent
Could not see where things went wrong
He packed his bags to see his Father
Went back Home where love was strong

Mom she cooked him hearty meal
Dad he listened before did speak
"Listen Son your ideas are good ones
But just don't treat all others meek"

"They too have Brains and understanding
They tend to switch off when feel insulted
Pitch your thoughts with them as equals
Equals you listen to and are consulted"

The Aspiring Man stayed Home a long time
Talked and listened to Mom and Dad
Learnt a lot about integration
Was best schooling he'd everhad

Time did come to strike out again
This time though with thought and care
Promoted ideas with different tact
Aspiring Man became millionaire

Aspiring Man became a model
A model of how things are done
For whilst you have dreams and aspirations
Remember that you are not the only one

BREATH AWAY

Many breathes are spent in growing
Many breathes in finding ME
Many breathes are spent in travel
Many breathes to where want to be

Life is not measured by the breathes you take but
by the moments that take your breath away.
Life is not measured accumulation of trinkets; Life is
measured in memories that don't fade but stay.

You take your breathes because you have to
You lose your breathe uncontrolled
You live your Life in search of some things
Some things leave you with stories told

Life is not measured in how many friendships,
but by friendships strong and true
Life is not measured by social standing but
by how you stand on being social

While you have breathe to takeaway
Let the breathe you take, mean and matter
From doing something for the first time
To softly listening to a young ones pitter patter

Let pleasures take your breath away
For a second let time stand still
When you see a sunrise somewhere special
Wish it a memory and it will

Become one of many that you have
That can recount of future day
When others listen to your Life story
Say with smile "it took my breath away"

———

MILK AND HONEY

You strip my reason with your actions
You make me ask the reason why
Then you are there and all is answered
Then I know the answer why

Times are hard in both lives
Distance means can't hold your hand
Does not mean that I don't miss you
Does not mean I don't understand

So my impulse is quickly quashed
Replaced with a senility
Frustration is so soon gone
Still you stay that part of me

Time will prove my love for you
For there is no greater test
My intentions are so sincere
With that inside am at your behest

Miss your talk when it is gone
Miss the giggle when you don't laugh
Miss the hearts on your replies
Miss those twists in our path

Right is my reason for caring
For is you that owns my heart
So endure all the challenges
For when we speak we make a start

I cannot promise a life of riches
For not rich in sense of money
But if care and worship were currency
We'd be rich in Milk and Honey

———

BECAUSE OF YOU

To this place I come to thank
The William's, Fred's, the Harry too
The Johns', the Peters', the Marks', the others
Those I live because of you
I have not much to offer but respect and gratitude
To each of you and those of kind
Our world now changes to allow those female
You're approving smile I think I'll find
So many ages upon this column
Both life years and years of life
Some passed alone, some with brothers
Some passed single, some with wife
How many years upon this tribute?
To those who stood and gave their all?
With dread yet sadness – for they are equal
One day will see Lady call
Turmoil it sits deep inside me
For when growing up I did learn
Fighting was a man ego hazard
The caring sex we shouldn't spurn
Doubt me not – you fallen heroes
Not because I think not able
More because will hit me harder
In this modern so unstable
I know with you they will be welcomed
As an equal in Family
Already seen some coffins carried
That did hit me forcibly
Equality is right and I am for it
Though growing up had no concept
That a sister, aunt or partner
Would be the ones that my freedom kept

Because of you – all of you
Courage knows no body made
Once your name is on this pillar
Then your story will never fade
Man or woman, whatever colour
You took the oath to us defend
That you are here where I am looking
Means in life you gave your end
Just how can we repay you?
Just how can we justify?
That so we can go on victimising
You stood up and you did die?
Fly forth you valiant spirits
May your views be peace and calm
In living I may not have known you
Thought in present you feel no harm
Walk tall for you're remembered
For us you gave your best
Because you were willing
We are beholden to pass our test
I come here when need direction
Just look at every name
I realise wars have consequences
They are not just some old game
Unlike you I'm not a soldier
For me that time has passed
You, however, will stay as warriors
Saw the thorn and then you grasped
I am no man that knows future places
Though a chance I freely take
If here I'm true and noble
Someday your hands I can then shake

CHILL

The gnawing seeps inside the core
Deeper and deeper does it go
On lighter skin a colour change
As red then blue does show

The wave of blissful relaxation
As slumped in favourite chair
Empty head and light heart
That comes with have no care

The immersion of your favourite drink
To sharpen clean crisp taste
Though improves upon the tongue
The aroma goes to waste

Cast down or demoralise
The dread of the effect
Sap morale and leave frail
The results that it gets

Personally I like two and three
They just go together
Not the chore of one and four
That comes with winter weather

A LIFE FULFILLED

A Life that's lived has many chapters
Some that change you, some make you stronger
One thing in Life guaranteed you
They'll be more chapters as it grows longer

Our youth is bliss, if we are lucky
Though memories made then they seem to go
Adolescence is a whirlpool
When all is chaos and we don't know

Sometimes I sit and self reflect. Sometimes laugh and
sometimes cry. Remember things long forgotten, remember
the good and relive the bad. I am guessing that this is
normal. Just has a personal unspoken rule. None like to
hear of your sadness. Turned to Art and that is Cool.

Amongst my memories I have a mixture
Within my Dreams one is clear
Triggered thoughts are sense of cleansing
To open up to loved ones dear

A Life Fulfilled will be indeed
When plans and dreams, they come together
When can banish the parts that I regret
Recount the good in better weather

As body changes so do expectations. Gone Bravado of the young.
Getting old is not so bad considering all that you have seen and
done. Just keep reaching seems the secret, never take for granted
what you have gained. Perhaps it is something you don't deserve.
Life is like that, sometimes strange. Good or bad our experiences,
one thing they do is they teach. There might be richer, more

intelligent, that don't mean happiness is out of reach. When is right time to plan for tomorrow? Well in truth was yesterday. Today, however, you are still breathing. The harvest of Life is still out there waiting. Pack your tools and make your Hay.

I came, I conquered
Sometimes retreated but tactical
I live and learn a Life Fulfilled
I have ambitious, my dreams are all

All that I need to keep me going
All that I need to make me strong
All that I need to plan my future
All that I need to go where I belong

SUNKEN SEEDS

Time moves on, it stops for no man
Love and passion are swept along
Caught in currents of the present
Stuck in silt if not that strong

New seeds fall into the river
Join the journey of random path
Some will crash on hidden boulders
Some avoid and will last

Sunken seeds are of many
Unknown the journey when begun
Not through choice but random futures
Fell to river and came undone

For love like nature ever evolving
Always adapts to carry on
Climates change as do seasons
Still the friendship stays so strong

Some plant their roots in fertile ground
Take nourishment from what is there
Spread and bloom in times passage
Have endurance when right is there

Then growth becomes a thing eternal
Always change and rearrange
Then one day a bud it grows
For the seed adapts so strange

The tree of life has so many seeds
Some do drown and some do grow
Still they fall into the river
Who knows which? We'll never know

CAN YOU SEE?

Can you see your common error?
Can you spot your personal trait?
Will you adapt and see this through
Will recognise but alas too late

Compartment thinking – everything has label
Compartment thinking – all has place
Compartment thinking – no grey areas
Compartment thinking – neatness has no space

The pollen seed floated helpless, travelling to where did not
know. Carried on the thermals high, dipping on depressions low.
Lottery is a pollen life, no choice in where that it will land.
How it fares it has some say, how much say in others hand.

Can you see yet where this is leading?
Can you see comparison made?
Will you look and just forget this
Will you notice efforts made

Compartment thinking – everything has label
Compartment thinking – all has place
Compartment thinking – no grey areas
Compartment thinking – neatness has no space

The atom bounced within the cell – protons /
neutrons, each did pull. That, however, is science
talking. We are science but not science all.
We need science to keep us healthy, amino acids and
vitamins. We need more thought than just existing –
need free thinking and what that brings.
I do think therefore I am. I am intelligent therefore I can.

228

Even complex is the structure of the one called 'simple man'. Simple Man is more intellectual, simple man does not just file. Simple man absorbs without influence, simple man learns with a smile.

Can you say with true conviction?
Can you say you hadn't prejudged this?
Will you be honest and learn the lesson
Will you discover the 'Free Think' bliss

WHEN ELDERS SPEAK

When elders speak they speak with wisdom
Speak of lessons some hard earned
When elders speak - they speak to teach you
Often lessons ignored and spurned

Elders make a pact with Fate
Pass on warnings before too late
Elders speak of wrong direction
Though your path is your conception

When time comes and you have young ones
Then understand what they did leak
Try your best to teach your loved sons
Then you talk in elders speak

When elders speak it's because they care
For is a bad old world out there
To protect and care for you
Elders speak - it's what they do

When Elders speak we should listen
For they know of things we do not know
Lived a life that was full of changes
Have a wisdom that's not on show

ANGELS RODE ON HORSEBACK

When Angels rode on Horseback
The ground it shook and Faith did cry
For both armies believing there's was Righteous
Never did allowance try
Hot heads both sides
Did fury whip
Though were minority
They were the tip
Blows exchanged, the passions changed
War cries rose from what was quip
The Faithful like Families took their sides
Sometimes is what families do
Get involved with one sides reasons
Of whole facts they have no clue
Some relatives commit atrocities
So whole religion does get the blame
Psychopath sect are ecstatic
When reaction does suit their game
The bold and brave strap on their armour
Saddle up and then ride out
Create the vacuum that sucks in others
Ride to glory with scream and shout
Been here before in our History
Victories gained but nothing changes
We've moved on with weapons and tactics
Though not to point that rearranges
So innocent once more will pay the blood bill
Fantasists will flock to join their banners
That is us in a nutshell
Gone are wisdom and gone good manners
So many aggrieved at outside influence
When upset at things at Home

Cost of living and future prospects
Hear a preacher and choose to roam
Though that preacher has agendas
For live in same world but have solution
Politics is hard, Religion easy
Both though ripe for revolution
Self styled Angels once rode on Horseback
Plundered, slaughtered for a name
We have developed so we say so
Why do we still enjoy this game?

CARRY ME ALONG

The man strolled down on golden beach
Felt the sand between his toes
Gazes out to a new horizon
So much different from that he knows

The water here a different colour
Somehow reflects his change of life
Silent standing, patient waiting
Smiling gently is his Wife

This view to her it is common
From early age she's viewed this scene
This is Home, this is her Home
Despite her travelling always has been

In an eye blink a world can change
In a heartbeat all is strange
In the snap of a finger click
Makes or breaks a wall so thick
In the crash of a cymbal hit
In that fraction of a bullet bit
In that prick of a needle stuck
Can gain a goal through work or luck

The woman watched quite contented
A gentle breeze through her long black hair
All she dreamed and all she wanted
Was before her just right there

He marvelled at how decisive
A change of thinking, it could be
He had found a Pearl to be his own
In fact had found two, found them in a far off sea

———

In an eye blink a world can change
In a heartbeat all is strange
In the snap of a finger click
Makes or breaks a wall so thick
In the crash of a cymbal hit
In that fraction of a bullet bit
In that prick of a needle stuck
Can gain a goal through work or luck

The Daughter swam in the shallows
Happy that all were together
Rising and dipping with the breakers
Hoping this would last forever

All is beautiful in this picture
All are at where they belong
It may for now be just a Daydream
Please Daydreaming carry me along

BE THIS WAY

A satirical look at modern life

The Policeman takes
The Medics drink
The Judges tied
Offenders think
Guess it is just this way
Politicians play to win their game
The abusers stake their claim
Companies ethics overruled game station nation has been fooled
Welcome to the new way
By the way are words of play
Only old ones do now say
All possible if we ignore
Some silly things called Rules of Law
Now it is the New Way
Got my wires and got my hub
Of the ethics a two bit rub
Was taught to seek what I am able
So spliced into next doors cable
Charity shops have no need to be
In my world they're all charity
Take objection? – overruled
Blade in pocket had you fooled
I am doing things my way
Get over it you pompous ass
Your times over and put to grass
We are your future and no one's fools
We look at screens so know what's cool
Have fingers so can hit that switch
If that thing happens you call a glitch
All is sorted in our way

———

Excuse me now for things to do
Gas and water's gone to poo
Transport sucks and Health care nil
Lucky can get this street sold pill
I am loving my way

WHEN ANGELS FLY

So what happens when Angels fly?
When spread their wings and do move on
Is it because we are whole again?
Is it they receive a lovers song?

Angels care when we are wanting
Angels watch when you believe
Silent guardians of your heart
Filter out those that deceive

When we are hurting an Angel flies
To repair and make us calm
Though it feeds on your belief
A rejected Angel feels the harm

So an Angel battered soars away
To lick its wounds for another friend
You no longer believe in Angels
Nor the friendship I try to send

No Angel me, that is true
Because of things did and things I do
Though I know but know not why
When we deceive is when Angels fly

CAN IT BE?

Years ago when love was created
Did they realise or have a clue
That many years later it would describe
This special feeling I feel for you
Can it be that life is perfect?
Have I now found my release?
All my tensions, fears and worries
Have now gone and am at peace
When you tell me that you love me
Nothing else matters any more
When you smile that special smile in my direction
I look into your eyes forever Mon amour

Your soul looks back with hope and loving
Tells me OK, relax awhile longer
I'll still be here when you awaken
I'll still be here and we'll be stronger
Throughout the time of recorded history
Many a romance written or put to song
They are nice but fail in comparison
To this feeling that we belong
The artist may have expressed it better
For I'm a man of simple word
Though to compare love by ones expression
It is a judgment quite absurd

So May-ari ng aking puso please forgive me
If this doesn't quite compare
For I am not quite well enough educated
To express what it means that you are there
Can it be that this journey's over
This Traveller's found his Home
For I have lost my will to wander
Lost that urge to roam
On far off shore sat my Lovebird
Her call so bright and clear
Caused me to change direction
To get her oh so near

Now my Lovebird is within touching distance
With tears of joy I silent weep
For with her is a child I call my own
A Family to love and keep

BEE

If I was the Bee that I want to be
Would I be a Bee with empathy?
The Bee that be the one to see
What Bee I be in reality

Would I be the Bee that be?
Nurtured, kept so lovingly
Or be a Bee you want to be
Be the spur for ability

Whatever Bee that I be
I be a Bee of morality
Bee that be of loyalty
That's the Bee that I do be

So the moral you can see
Is we can be what want to be
Be a person you wish to be
Me I'm happy, I be a Bee

ALCOHOLIC ATTITUDES

Bradley was a Beer drinker
Found courage when was drunk
Braver did our Bradley get
In ratio to what had sunk

Candy into Cocktails
She thinks that they are cool
Pour enough into her
She'll let you use your tool

Alcohol makes many changes
Some crazy things they do
Some do want to fight the World
Some think they love you true

How many do remember
When they wake the next day
How they acted night before
What damage they did say?

Some they do grow out of it
Some do like that scene
They are the ones in later life
Regret what might have been
A Gift for Gie and Another for anak Mj

A Gift for 'Gie' so that she can see
Just how much she means to me
Another for anak Mj to say
She lights our World and makes our Day
Two Books one cover for Daughter and Mother
I love them both as I could love no other

My Gifts for you are my Heart and Soul
My words and vacant time
To have found you both and then to lose
For me the worst of crimes

What I do is for you to see
That one a soul mate, one legacy
Both are jewels in my Life's crown
When they're about I can't feel down
A look, a voice, something they play
Lightens my and makes my day
Time itself can bring rewards
I was patient and got Two
My Life has changed and for the better
My Life has turned into something new
The Mother is a keeper
A Daughter I won't let go
They have been, done so much before
Some yet that I don't know

Yet still they welcomed into their bond
This stranger, I don't know why
Welcomed me and accepted me
Was so honoured I could cry
So now we are a three piece band
One musician and duo
Each has different taste in music
That lap and overflow

To Follow:
Messages for Mj